Easy Beaded Crochet

Carol Meldrum

SEARCH PRESS

A QUARTO BOOK

Published in 2006 by Search Press Ltd.
Wellwood
North Farm Road
Tunbridge Wells
Kent
TN2 3DR

ISBN-13: 978-1-84448-144-6
ISBN-10: 1-84448-144-1

QUAR.EBC

Conceived, designed and produced by
Quarto Publishing plc
The Old Brewery
6 Blundell Street
London N7 9BH

Project Editor Donna Gregory
Art Editor Julie Joubinaux
Designer Louise Clements
Photographer Sam Sloan
Photographer's Assistant Alan McRedie
Models Laura Caird, Claire Lithgow,
Gillian Cook, and Nikki Goodwin
Stylist Joanna Outhwaite
Illustrator Kate Simunek
Pattern Checker Christine Ticknor
Indexer Dorothy Frame
Assistant Art Director Penny Cobb

Art Director Moira Clinch
Publisher Paul Carslake

Colour separation by
Universal Graphics Pte Ltd, Singapore
Printed by
SNP Leefung Printers Limited, China

Contents

Introduction 8

Materials, tools and techniques 10

Materials 12

Beads 14

Tools 16

Getting started 18

Basic stitches 21

Working in rounds 25

Shaping techniques 26

Lace work 28

Understanding patterns 30

Tension 31

Finishing techniques 32

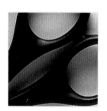

continued
on next page ▶

Quick-and-easy projects

Beaded ruffle scarf **38**

Shoulder bag **48**

Beaded beret **60**

Lace-effect shawl **40**

Evening bag **52**

Textured beaded bag **64**

Wrist warmers **42**

Flower pin corsage **54**

Beaded necklace **66**

Pashmina **44**

Beaded beanie **56**

Earflap hat **68**

Beaded string bag **46**

Twenties-inspired scarf **58**

Beaded head band **70**

Brooch and pendant **72**

Beaded tunic **88**

Beaded throw **108**

Box crew-neck **76**

Bikini top **91**

Circular motif cushion **110**

Slash-neck top **80**

Cap-sleeved wrap **94**

Beaded mat **112**

Halter-neck top **83**

Motifs for sweaters **98**

Floor cushion **114**

Cobweb shrug **86**

Appliqué cushion **104**

Coasters **118**

Trims **120**
Yarn directory **122**
Resources **124**
Index and credits **127**

introduction

Over the past few years we have seen the interest in all aspects of crochet increase tremendously. Catwalk designers are incorporating this craft into their collections and the influx of crochet into the high-street shops has really had an impact. Crochet is once again seen as being cool and hip. Traditional techniques and patterns are enjoying a new lease of life.

As the title of this book suggests, I have concentrated on beaded crochet. Beads are no longer just for trims and accents – we can play about and put them all over. There are no hard-and-fast rules when it comes to which beads or sequins to use: they just have to be big enough to fit on the yarn, or if they are too small, simply stitch them into place.

There is something for everybody – scarves, bags, hats, jewellery, projects for the home, as well as modern classic garments like the cap-sleeved wrap-over cardigan and the cobweb shrug. Each technique is fully explained and illustrated, providing you with everything you need to get started. All projects are written in the form of easy-to-follow patterns, with step-by-step instructions on any new skills required to complete a particular project, and clear photographs of what the finished piece will look like.

Choose from a wide range of inspired and original simple projects to spark the imagination and to give you the confidence to be creative with beads. Have fun working with a wide variety of yarns from 2-ply mohairs to super-chunky wools for fast, effective results. So pick up your hook, choose your beads, and get started!

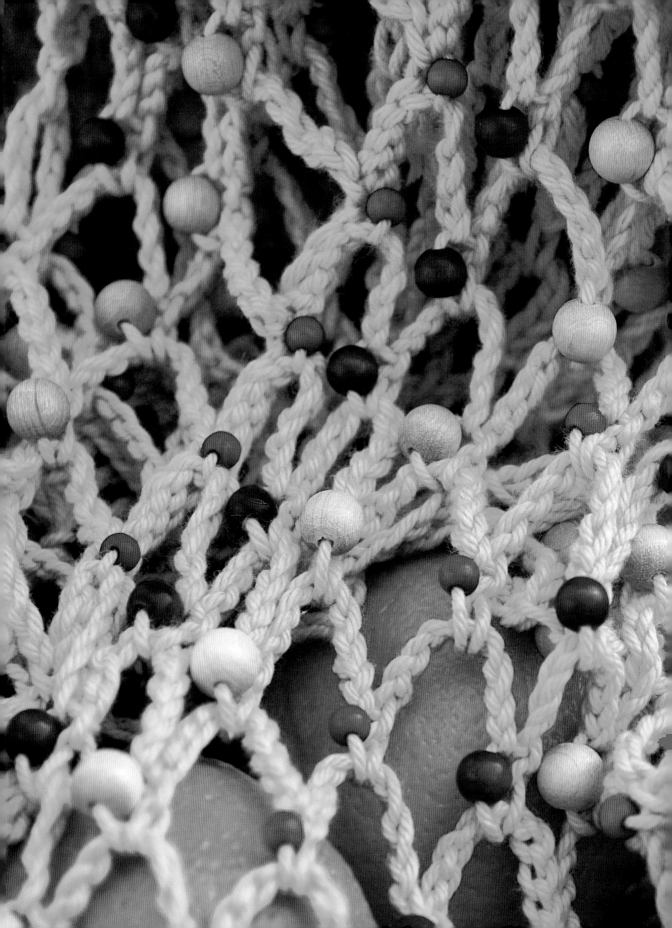

Materials, tools and Techniques

Materials

You can create a crochet fabric from almost any continuous length of fibre, but yarn is the most commonly used material. Yarns for crochet come in a wide variety of fibres, weights, colours, and price ranges, and it is important to choose the right yarn to suit your project. Although the specific yarns used to make the projects are listed on pages 122–123, you may wish to crochet a project using a different yarn. Understanding the qualities of the various types of yarn available will help you choose one that is suitable. Beads and sequins are a great way to add colour to your crochet. They can give a funky feel or a touch of sophistication. Beads are available in a wide range of shapes, sizes, materials and colours.

Yarn

Yarns are usually made by spinning together different types of fibres. The fibres may be natural materials obtained from animals or plants, for example wool or cotton, or they can be manmade fibres such as nylon or acrylic. Yarns may be made from one fibre or combine a mixture of two or three different ones in varying proportions. Several fine strands of yarn (called "plies") are often twisted together to make thicker weights of yarn. Novelty yarns, such as tweeds and other textured

SILK

COTTON

MOHAIR

WOOL

Yarns are made from many different raw materials, and each kind has advantages and disadvantages. Animal fibres (wool is the most common) are soft, warm, relatively expensive and keep their shape well, though some of the more expensive kinds, such as silk, cashmere or mohair are not very resilient. Vegetable fibres, such as cotton, are durable and cool to wear, but cotton and linen yarns are often prone to shrinkage. Synthetic yarns (such as nylon, polyester and acrylic) are usually cheaper, stable, machine-washable and less prone to shrinkage, but they can lose their shape when heat is applied.

yarns, combine several strands of different weights and textures twisted together.

Metallic and ribbon yarns are constructed by knitting very fine yarn into tubes and giving them a rounded or flattened appearance. As a general rule, the easiest yarns to use for crochet, especially for a beginner, have a smooth surface and a medium or tight twist. These are also the best yarns to use with beads.

Yarn is sold by weight rather than by length, although the packaging of many yarns does include length per ball as well as other information. The length of yarn in the ball will vary according to thickness and fibre composition. It is usually packaged into balls, although some yarns may come in the form of hanks or skeins that need to be wound by hand into balls before you can begin to crochet.

Ball bands

The yarn you buy will have a band around it that lists lots of important information, including company brand and yarn name, weight and length of yarn, fibre content, shade and dye lot numbers, recommended needle or hook size, tension and washing instructions. See glossary at the back of the book for explanations of these terms.

COMPANY BRAND AND YARN NAME

WEIGHT AND LENGTH

WASHING INSTRUCTIONS

TENSION

FIBRE CONTENT

NEEDLE SIZE

SHADE AND DYE LOT NUMBERS

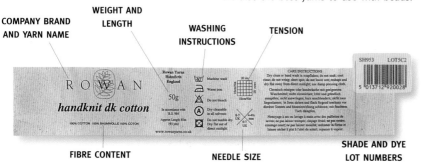

Buttons

Buttons can make or break a project, so it is worth spending a little more for an interesting button that will enhance your crochet piece. Wooden buttons are used for the projects in this book, though shell or pearlized buttons could also work. Always buy buttons after working the buttonholes to ensure a good fit.

Jewellery wire

Yarn is not the only material you can crochet with. Bracelets, necklaces and even earrings can be made from a reel of jewellery wire. Beads can be threaded directly onto the wire without using a needle even when the wire is soft and flexible enough to crochet. Thick wires are more difficult to crochet than thin wires.

Other materials

Other materials used to make the projects in this book include cushion pads, zips, stuffing and jewellery fastenings. These can all be purchased from good haberdashery shops.

Yarn weights

Yarns are available in a range of thicknesses, referred to as weights, varying from very fine to very chunky. Although each weight of yarn is described by a specific name, there may actually be a lot of variation in the thicknesses when yarns are produced by different manufacturers or in different countries. There are lots of sorts of beads available nowadays; from wooden to plastic, from glass to bone, and many more besides, but it is vital to consider how well your chosen bead and yarn will go together before finalizing your choice. Use this simple checklist to guide you:

1 Will the yarn fit through the centre of the bead?

2 Do the bead and yarn have similar washing requirements? High temperatures will tarnish most beads.

3 Is the bead a suitable weight for the yarn? If it is too heavy, the crocheted fabric will distort; if it is too light and small, the bead may seem lost in the yarn.

The most commonly used weights of yarn, including those used in this book, are:

sport/4-ply	• Fine yarns that are usually crocheted on hook sizes 12–9 (2.5–3.5 mm).
double knitting (dk)	• Slightly less than twice the thickness of sport or 4-ply yarns, usually crocheted on hook sizes 9–7 (3.5–4.5 mm).
worsted	• Just under twice the thickness of dk, crocheted on hook sizes 6–4 (5–6 mm).
aran	• Also just under twice the thickness of dk and crocheted on hook sizes 6–4 (5–6 mm).
bulky	• Any chunky yarn that is thicker than worsted or Aran, crocheted on hook sizes 4–2 (6–7 mm).
super bulky	• Really fat yarns, variously termed extra bulky, super bulky or extra super bulky, crocheted on hook sizes 1 (8 mm) upwards.

LINEN

VISCOSE/POLYESTER

Beads

Central to every project in this book is the use of beads, which add a glamorous touch to crocheted garments and are great for embellishing accessories. Whether worked into the fabric during knitting or sewn on afterwards, they can be used to create a range of effects – use them sparingly to create a subtle look, or liberally for a more dramatic effect.

Beads are made from a variety of materials, including plastic, bone and wood, but the majority of the projects in this book use glass beads because of the richness of colour they create.

When choosing beads, check whether they are machine washable. Also make sure that they are an appropriate size for the yarn you are using. For example, do not use large glass beads with a sport-weight yarn because they will cause the crochet to sag; similarly, avoid using very small beads with bulky-weight yarn because the beading will not stand out enough and the beads may slip through the stitches to the wrong side of the fabric, especially if it is not knitted very tightly.

Always make sure that the hole in the centre of the bead is big enough to pass a doubled end of yarn through. When knitting with two ends of yarn at the same time, thread the beads onto the finer yarn, hold the ends of both yarns together and work as normal.

Seed beads

These small, round glass beads are ideal for embellishing knitted fabrics. They can be sewn onto the finished item, but are also very easy to incorporate into the fabric during knitting. Seed beads are available in a wide variety of sizes and in many different finishes. Some are made with coloured glass, while others are transparent and lined with colour, which means that the central hole has been painted with colour. Seed beads are commonly sold by gram weight.

Decorative beads

As well as using seed beads, the projects in this book feature a variety of other decorative beads. Some of the more common types of bead are bugles (long, thin, cylinder-shaped beads), cubes, triangles, daggers and Magatamas (teardrop). A quick browse through a bead shop, catalogue or website will also reveal beads in the shape of leaves, flowers, faces, fish, bicones, crystals, stars... The list goes on and on, and all of these beads are beautiful. When choosing beads for crochet projects, remember to check that the hole is an appropriate size for your yarn, and that the bead itself is quite smooth (inside and out), or it will damage your finished article. If used for garments (as opposed to jewellery or accessories), odd-shaped beads may be uncomfortable for the wearer.

Glass beads are available in a wide range of colours and sizes.

There are lots of different kinds of decorated beads, such as these Kenyan ceramic beads.

TIP: BUYING BEADS

Even if a pattern or book project states exactly how many beads are required, it is always best to buy more than specified if possible. This is particularly important with small seed beads. You may have to discard some beads as you work, perhaps because they are sharp-edged or misshapen, or you may break or lose some. Beads are made and dyed in batches, so if you have to buy more beads to finish a piece, you may well find that the new beads vary in colour from those in the rest of the project. It may also take some time before your bead stockist has more supplies, or a colour may occasionally be discontinued.

Keep beads in shallow containers while you are working with them.

There is a huge array of compartmentalized boxes for storing your beads, and these are invaluable both for storing your beads in, and for keeping your colours separate when working on a project.

Choosing beads

The sheer variety of colours, sizes and finishes of beads can be bewildering. Here is a handy guide to help you to decide which bead you should choose for your project.

Sizing

Beads come in a variety of sizes. Glass seed beads, which are perfect for incorporating into crochet designs, are most often sold in size 11/0, though be aware that sizes may vary slightly between manufacturers. Using beads of different sizes within one piece can cause the tension to vary, so it is better to keep the beads all the same size.

Colours

Made from glass, seed beads come in a stunning range of colours, finishes and sizes. You can find a colour to suit every design, and they are more than a little addictive!

The beads themselves can be:

Transparent – made of clear glass so you can see right through the bead.

Translucent – the glass is slightly milky, so light can still pass through it.

Opaque – the glass is a solid colour, and light cannot pass through it.

Silver-lined – the hole at the centre of the bead has a mirror-like lining, making the bead sparkle.

Colour-lined – the hole through the centre of the bead is lined with a different colour.

Satin – the glass is striated, giving an effect like the mineral tiger's-eye, or satin fabric.

Finishes

As well as colour, a finish can also be applied to the surface of the bead, such as:

AB – *Aurora borealis*. A clear rainbow finish over the bead, similar to that seen on oil in water.

Iris – an iridescent finish applied to an opaque glass bead, giving it a metallic look.

Lustre – a shiny finish. This can be clear, coloured or metallic – for example, gold lustre beads which have a lovely warm glow. An opaque lustered bead is called "pearl" and a translucent lustered bead is called "ceylon".

Matte – the glass is etched, giving a soft, frosted finish.

Metallic/galvanized – a metal finish or coating applied to the bead. Although some of these can last well, this finish can wear off with handling.

Painted/dyed – some beads are painted or dyed. Although these beads are beautiful, paint can wear off when the beads are handled or it can fade in sunlight.

Wooden beads can be stained, painted, varnished or natural.

Pearls can be used to crochet with, and will add a sophisticated touch to any garment.

Some of these Czech matte glass beads have a special *Aurora Borealis* (AB) finish.

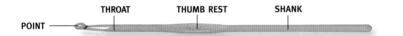

ALUMINIUM AND RESIN HOOKS

Tools

Very little equipment is needed for crochet – all you really require is a hook, although items such as pins and sharp scissors are useful and relatively inexpensive. The tools mentioned here are the basics; others can be bought as you go along.

Hooks

Crochet hooks are available in a wide range of sizes, shapes and materials. The most common sorts of hooks used for working with the types of yarns covered in this book are made from aluminium or plastic. Small sizes of steel hooks are also made for working crochet with very fine cotton yarns. (This type of fine yarn is known as crochet thread.) Some brands of aluminium and steel hooks have plastic handles to give a better grip (often called "soft touch" handles) and make the work easier on the fingers. Handmade wooden and horn hooks are also available, many featuring decorative handles. Bamboo hooks are great to work with because they are made from a natural material and have a very smooth finish.

Crochet hooks come in a range of sizes, from very fine to very thick. Finer yarns usually require a smaller hook, thicker yarns a larger hook. There appears to be no standardization of hook sizing between manufacturers. The points and throats of different brands of hooks often vary in shape, which affects the size of stitch they produce.

Hook sizes are quoted differently in Europe and the US, and some brands of hooks are labelled with more than one type of numbering. The hook sizes quoted in pattern instructions are a useful guide, but you may find that you need to use smaller or larger hook sizes, depending on the brand, to achieve the correct tension for the pattern (see page 31).

Choosing a hook is largely a matter of personal preference and will depend on various factors such as hand size, finger length, weight of hook, and whether you like the feel of aluminium or plastic in your hand. The most important things to consider when choosing a hook is how it feels in your hand and the ease with which it works with your yarn. When you have found your perfect brand of hook, it is useful to buy a range of several different sizes. Store your hooks in a clean container – you can buy a fabric roll with loops to secure the hooks, or use a zip-up purse such as a cosmetic bag.

POINT — THROAT — THUMB REST — SHANK

Comparative crochet hook sizes (from smallest to largest)

UK	US	METRIC (MM)	UK	US	METRIC (MM)
6	14	0.60	14		2.00
5½	13		13		
5	12	0.75	12	B	2.50
4½	11		11	C	3.00
4	10	1.00	10	D	
3½	9		9	E	3.50
3	8	1.25	8	F	4.00
2½	7	1.50	7	G	4.50
2	6	1.75	6	H	5.00
1½	5		5	I	5.50
1	4	2.00	4	J	6.00
1/0	3		2	K	7.00
2/0	2	2.50	1	L	8.00
3/0	1	3.00	0	N	9.00
	0		00	P	10.0000 3.50

Markers

Split rings or shaped loops made from brightly coloured plastic can be slipped onto your crochet to mark a place on a pattern, to indicate the beginning row of a repeat, and to help with counting the stitches on the foundation chain.

MARKERS

Sewing needles

Tapestry needles have blunt points and long eyes and are normally used for counted thread embroidery. They come in a range of sizes and are used for weaving in yarn ends and for sewing pieces of crochet together. Very large blunt-pointed needles are often labelled as "yarn needles". You may also need a selection of sewing needles with sharp points for applying crochet edging, working embroidery stitches and so on.

SEWING NEEDLES

Tape measure

Choose one that shows both centimetres and inches on the same side and replace it when it becomes worn or frayed because this means it will probably have stretched and become inaccurate. A 30-cm (12-in.) metal or plastic ruler is also useful for measuring tension swatches.

TAPE MEASURE

Pins

Glass-headed rustproof pins are the best type to use for blocking (see pages 32–33). Plastic-headed or pearl-headed pins can be used for pinning crochet and for cold-water blocking, but do not use this type for warm-steam blocking because the heat of the iron will melt the plastic heads. Quilters' long pins with fancy heads are useful when pinning pieces of crochet together because the heads are easy to see and will not slip through the crochet fabric.

Row counter

A knitter's row counter will help you keep track of the number of rows you have worked, or you may prefer to use a notebook and pencil.

ROW COUNTER

GLASS-HEADED PINS

QUILTERS' PINS

SHARP SCISSORS

Notebook

Keep a small notebook handy to record where you are in the pattern or any changes you have made.

Sharp scissors

Choose a small, pointed pair to cut yarn and trim off yarn ends.

Sewing thread

This is used to thread the beads onto the yarn.

SEWING THREAD

Getting started

The first step when beginning to crochet is to create a foundation chain of loops. It is also important to hold the hook and yarn correctly. There are numerous ways of doing this, but the best method is the one that feels most comfortable to you.

Holding the hook

There are a few different methods of holding the hook and yarn. There is no right or wrong way. The most important thing is to use the method that you prefer and the type of hook that you find most comfortable.

Pen hold

Hold the hook as if it were a pen, with the tips of your thumb and forefinger over the flat section or middle of the hook.

Knife hold

Hold the hook as if it were a knife, almost grasping the flat section or middle of the hook between your thumb and forefinger.

Holding the yarn

It is important to wrap the yarn around your fingers to control the supply of yarn and to keep the tension even. You can hold the yarn in several ways, but again it is best to use the method that feels the most comfortable.

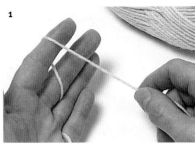

1

1 Loop the short end of the yarn over your forefinger, with the yarn coming from the ball under the next finger. Grip the length of yarn coming from the ball gently with your third and little fingers.

2

2 Alternatively, loop the short end of the yarn over your forefinger, with the yarn coming from the ball under your next two fingers and then wrapped around the little finger.

Making a slip knot

All crochet is made up from one loop on the hook at any time. The first working loop begins as a slip knot. The first loop does not count as a stitch.

1

1 Take the short end of the yarn in one hand and wrap it around the forefinger on your other hand.

2

2 Slip the loop off your forefinger and push a loop of the short end of the yarn through the loop from your forefinger.

3

3 Insert the hook into this second loop. Gently pull the short end of the yarn to tighten the loop around the hook and complete the slip knot.

Foundation chains

From the slip knot, you can now create a foundation chain (this is similar to casting on in knitting). This chain determines the width of the work.

1

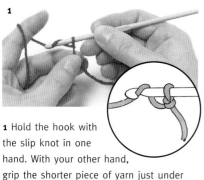

1 Hold the hook with the slip knot in one hand. With your other hand, grip the shorter piece of yarn just under the slip knot with your thumb and middle finger, and hold the longer piece of yarn over the forefinger. To create the first chain stitch, use your forefinger to wrap the yarn over the hook (known as "yarn over").

2

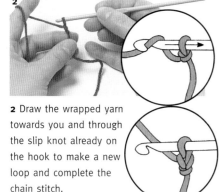

2 Draw the wrapped yarn towards you and through the slip knot already on the hook to make a new loop and complete the chain stitch.

3

3 Repeat this process, remembering to move your thumb and middle finger up the chain as it lengthens. When counting the chain stitches, each V-shaped loop on the front of the chain counts as one, except the one on the hook, which is known as a working stitch.

Beaded foundation chain

Incorporating beads into the foundation chain is very easy to do.

1

1 Make a slip knot in the usual way, then bring a bead up to the top of the yarn, place the bead under the hook and wrap the yarn over the hook.

2

2 Pull the yarn through the loop, leaving the bead at the front of the work, lying on the chain. Continue in this way for each beaded chain stitch required in the pattern.

TIP: COUNTING STITCHES

The front of the chain looks like a series of V shapes, while the back of the chain forms a distinctive "bump" of yarn behind each V shape. When counting chain stitches, count each V shape on the front of the chain as one chain stitch, except for the chain stitch on the hook, which is not counted. You may find it easier to turn the chain over and count the "bumps" on the back of the chain.

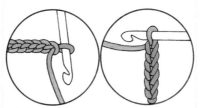

Adding beads and sequins

It is easy to incorporate beads and sequins into crochet fabrics. Any type of beads and sequins can be used, provided that the central hole is large enough for the yarn to pass through. See pages 14–15 for ideas.

1

1 Thread a sewing needle with a short length of sewing cotton and knot the ends. Pass the yarn through the loop made. Slide each bead or sequin onto the needle, then down the sewing cotton and onto the yarn. Pull the yarn through and continue threading on beads or sequins in this way.

2

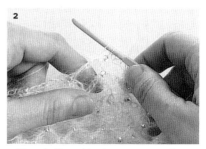

2 When indicated in the pattern, push a bead or sequin up the yarn to sit just below the crochet hook. Work the next stitch as instructed – in this case, double crochet – leaving the bead or sequin at the front of the work.

Working into the foundation chain

The first row of stitches is worked into the foundation chain. There are two ways of doing this, with the first method being easiest for the beginner.

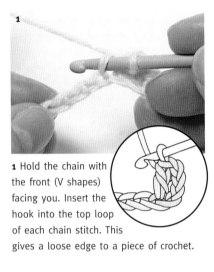

1 Hold the chain with the front (V shapes) facing you. Insert the hook into the top loop of each chain stitch. This gives a loose edge to a piece of crochet.

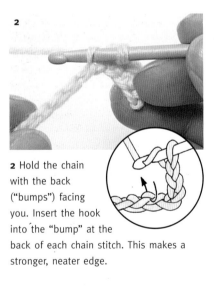

2 Hold the chain with the back ("bumps") facing you. Insert the hook into the "bump" at the back of each chain stitch. This makes a stronger, neater edge.

Turning chains

When working crochet, you need to work a specific number of extra chain stitches at the beginning of a row or round. These stitches are called a turning chain when worked at the beginning of a straight row and a starting chain when worked at the beginning of a round. What they do is bring the hook up to the correct height for the next stitch to be worked, so the longer the stitch, the longer the turning chain that is necessary.

The patterns in this book specify how many chain stitches need to be worked at the beginning of a row or round. The list below shows the standard number of chain stitches needed to make a turn for each type of basic crochet stitch, but a pattern may vary from this in order to produce a specific effect. If you have a tendency to work chain stitches very tightly, you may need to work an extra chain stitch in order to keep the edges of your work from becoming too tight.

Number of turning chain stitches

- Double crochet = 1 turning chain
- Extended double crochet = 2 turning chains
- Half treble crochet = 2 turning chains
- Treble crochet = 3 turning chains
- Double treble crochet = 4 turning chains

> **TIP: WORKING WITH TURNING CHAINS**
>
> The turning or starting chain is counted as the first stitch of the row except when working double crochet, when the turning chain is ignored. At the end of the row or round, the final stitch is usually worked into the turning or starting chain of the previous row or round.

Longer stitches, such as the treble crochet used to make this tunic (pages 88–90), require more turning chains than short stitches such as double crochet.

Basic stitches

Various stitches can be worked onto the foundation chain to form a crochet fabric. Each stitch gives a different texture and varies in depth.

TIP: NUMBER OF CHAINS

This diagram shows the number of chains from the hook. Different crochet stitches are worked a different number of chains from the hook. For example, double crochet is usually worked through the second chain from the hook, while treble crochet is worked through the fourth chain from the hook.

Double crochet (dc)

This is the easiest of crochet fabrics to create, producing a compact fabric that is still flexible.

1 Work the foundation chain plus one extra chain stitch (this is the turning chain). Insert the hook from front to back through the second chain from the hook. Wrap the yarn over the hook and draw the yarn through the chain towards you, leaving two loops on the hook.

3

3 Continue in this way along the row, working one double crochet stitch into each chain stitch.

2

2 Wrap the yarn over the hook again and draw it through both loops on the hook. This leaves one loop on the hook and completes the stitch.

4

4 At the end of the row, turn and work one chain for the turning chain. When working treble crochet back along the row, insert the hook from front to back under both loops of the double crochet stitches of the previous row.

Slip stitch (sl st)

This is commonly used to join ends of work together to form a ring or to work across the top of other stitches invisibly. Insert the hook from front to back into the last chain just worked. Wrap the yarn over the hook, then draw the yarn towards you through both the chain and the loop on the hook.

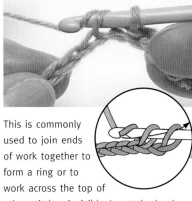

5

5 Fabric composed entirely of double crochet stitches is compact but flexible.

Extended double crochet (exdc)

As its name suggests, this stitch is slightly longer than a double crochet stitch.

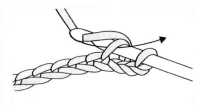

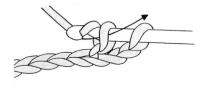

1 Work the foundation chain plus two extra chain stitches (this is the turning chain). Insert the hook from front to back through the third chain from the hook. Wrap the yarn over the hook and draw the yarn through the chain towards you, leaving two loops on the hook.

2 Wrap the yarn over the hook again and draw it through the first loop on the hook, again leaving two loops on the hook.

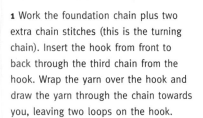

3 Wrap the yarn over the hook again and draw it through both loops on the hook.

4 This leaves one loop on the hook and completes the stitch. Continue in this way along the row, working one extended double crochet into each chain stitch.

At the end of the row, turn and work two chains for the turning chain. When working extended double crochet back along the row, insert the hook from front to back under both loops of the extended double crochet stitches of the previous row.

Treble crochet (tr)

Treble crochet is a longer stitch than double crochet, creating a more open and flexible fabric. The stitch is similar, except that you wrap the yarn over the hook before working into the fabric.

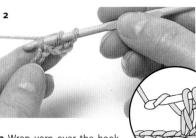

1 Work the foundation chain plus three extra chain stitches (this is the turning chain). Wrap the yarn over the hook, then insert the hook from front to back into the fourth chain from the hook.

2 Wrap yarn over the hook again and draw the yarn through the chain towards you, leaving three loops on the hook.

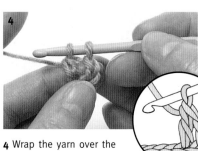

3 Wrap the yarn over the hook again and draw it through the first two loops, leaving two loops on the hook.

4 Wrap the yarn over the hook again and draw it through the last two loops.

5 This leaves one loop on the hook and completes the stitch. Continue in this way along the row, working one treble crochet into each chain stitch.

6 At the end of the row, turn and work three chains for the turning chain. When working treble crochet back along the row, skip the first treble crochet stitch at the beginning of the row and insert the hook from front to back through both loops of each remaining treble crochet stitches of the previous row. At the end of the row, work the last stitch into the top of the turning chain.

7 Fabric composed entirely of treble crochet stitches is still firm, like double crochet fabric, but slightly more open and flexible.

Half treble crochet (htr)
This stitch is slightly shorter than the treble crochet stitch.

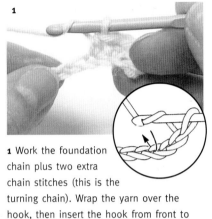

1 Work the foundation chain plus two extra chain stitches (this is the turning chain). Wrap the yarn over the hook, then insert the hook from front to back into the third chain from the hook.

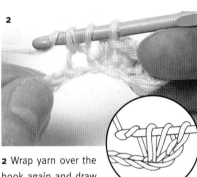

2 Wrap yarn over the hook again and draw the yarn through the chain towards you, leaving three loops on the hook. Wrap the yarn over the hook again and draw it through all three loops. This leaves one loop on the hook and completes the stitch.

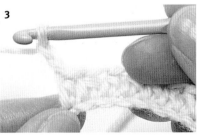

3 Continue in this way along the row, working one half treble crochet into each chain stitch. At the end of the row, turn and work two chains for the turning chain.

4 When working half treble crochet back along the row, skip the first half treble crochet stitch at the beginning of the row, then insert the hook from front to back under both loops of each remaining half treble crochet stitch of the previous row.

5 At the end of the row, work the last stitch into the top of the turning chain.

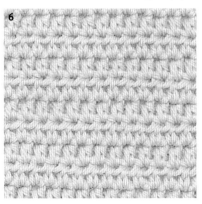

6 Fabric composed entirely of half treble crochet stitches is firm and flexible, but not as compact as double crochet or treble crochet fabric.

Double treble crochet (dtr)

This stitch is slightly longer than the treble crochet stitch.

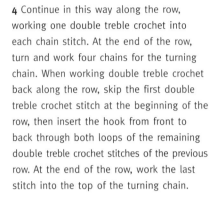

1 Work the foundation chain plus four extra chain stitches (this is the turning chain). Wrap the yarn over the hook twice, then insert the hook from front to back into the fifth chain from the hook. Wrap the yarn over the hook again and draw the yarn through the chain towards you, leaving four loops on the hook.

2 Wrap the yarn over the hook again and draw it through the first two loops, leaving three loops on the hook.

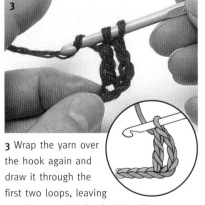

3 Wrap the yarn over the hook again and draw it through the first two loops, leaving two loops on the hook. Wrap the yarn over the hook again and draw it under the last two loops. This leaves one loop on the hook and completes the stitch.

4 Continue in this way along the row, working one double treble crochet into each chain stitch. At the end of the row, turn and work four chains for the turning chain. When working double treble crochet back along the row, skip the first double treble crochet stitch at the beginning of the row, then insert the hook from front to back through both loops of the remaining double treble crochet stitches of the previous row. At the end of the row, work the last stitch into the top of the turning chain.

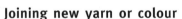

5 Fabric composed entirely of double treble crochet stitches is open and very flexible.

Joining new yarn or colour

It is best to join a new yarn at the end of a row, but you can join a new yarn anywhere in a row if you need to. Leave the last stage of the final stitch incomplete, loop the new yarn over the hook and use it to complete the stitch. Work the next row in the new yarn or colour. When changing colour in the middle of a row, begin the stitch in the usual way, wrap the new yarn over the hook, draw the new yarn through the stitch towards you and then work the stitch.

Working into front and back of stitches

It is usual to work crochet stitches under both loops of the stitches made on the previous row. However, sometimes a pattern will instruct you to work under just one loop, either the back or the front, in which case the remaining loop becomes a horizontal bar.

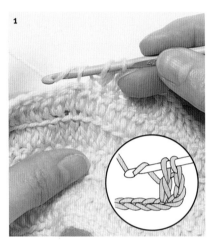

1 To work into the front of a row of stitches, insert the hook under only the front loops of the stitches on the previous row.

2 To work into the back of a row of stitches, insert the hook under only the back loops of the stitches on the previous row. Working into the back of the stitch creates a strongly ridged fabric.

Working in rounds

Some circular pieces of crochet require that you work in rounds rather than rows. The basic stitch techniques are the same, but you work around the work rather than back and forth.

Making a ring

To start, you have to make a ring by joining a small length of chain with a slip stitch. The chain is usually between 4 and 6 stitches, depending on the thickness of yarn being used.

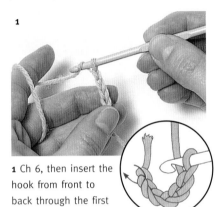

1 Ch 6, then insert the hook from front to back through the first chain made.

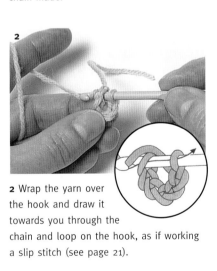

2 Wrap the yarn over the hook and draw it towards you through the chain and loop on the hook, as if working a slip stitch (see page 21).

3 Gently tighten the first stitch by pulling the loose yarn end. You have now created a ring of chains.

Working into the ring

The foundation ring is the centre of your circular crochet and where you will work into on the next round.

1 Depending on the stitch you will be using, make the appropriate length of starting chain (see page 20).

TIP: MARKING ROUNDS
Place a marker at the beginning of the round. This will help to show where the round stops and starts because sometimes it can be tricky to tell. Simply pull the marker out at the end of each round and reposition it for the next.

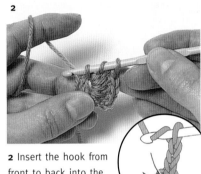

2 Insert the hook from front to back into the centre of the ring (not into the chain) for each stitch and work the number of stitches specified in the pattern. Remember when working in rounds that the right side is always facing you.

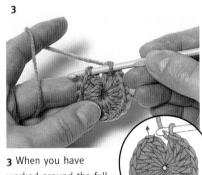

3 When you have worked around the full circle, finish off the round by working a slip stitch into the top of the starting chain worked at the beginning of the round.

Shaping techniques

Shaping your crochet is done by increasing or decreasing stitches along a row. When adding or subtracting stitches at intervals along a row, this is called internal increase or decrease. When stitches are added or subtracted at the beginning or end of a row, this is called external increase or decrease. Each method creates a different effect.

Internal increases

This is the simplest method of adding stitches at intervals along a row.

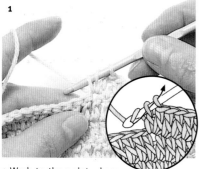

1 Work to the point where you want to increase, then work two or more stitches into one stitch on the previous row.

2 This method is often used one stitch in from the edge at the beginning and end of a row to shape garment edges neatly. At the beginning of the row, work the first stitch and then work the increase as described in step 1.

3 At the end of the row, work to the last two stitches, work the increase in the next to last stitch as described in step 1, and then work the last stitch.

External increases

This method can be used to increase several stitches at one time. You will need to add extra foundation chains at the beginning or end of a row.

1 To add stitches at the beginning of a row, work the required number of extra chains at the end of the previous row and remember to add the turning chains.

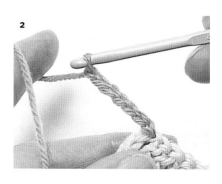

2 On the next row, work the extra stitches along the chain and then continue along the row.

3 To add stitches at the end of a row, leave the last few stitches of the row unworked. Remove the hook and join a length of yarn to the last stitch of the row and work the required number of extra foundation chains. Fasten off the yarn.

4 Place the hook back into the row, complete the row and then continue working the extra stitches across the chain.

Internal decreases

As with the internal increases, if you are decreasing stitches in order to create a neat edge when shaping, always work the decrease one stitch in from the edge.

External decreases

This method is best used if you want to decrease several stitches at one time.

1 The easiest way to decrease stitches across a row is simply to skip one stitch of the previous row.

3 The same method can also be used for decreasing more than two stitches. In this example, three stitches are decreased by working them together.

1 To decrease at the beginning of a row, work a slip stitch (see page 21) into each of the stitches that you want to decrease, then work the turning chains and continue along the row.

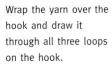

2 Alternatively, two stitches can be worked together. Start working the first stitch of the decrease but do not complete it; instead, leave two loops on the hook. Insert the hook into the next stitch and work another incomplete stitch so that you have three loops on the hook. Wrap the yarn over the hook and draw it through all three loops on the hook.

2 To decrease at the end of a row, leave the stitches to be decreased unworked. Work the turning chains, then turn and work along the next row.

Shaping techniques, used to make projects such as this ear-flap hat (pages 68–69), are easy to learn.

Lace work

Lace motifs are light, pretty and delicate to look at when worked in light-weight yarns, and are perfect for making shawls, wraps and stoles. It is usual to join several motifs to make a strip, then add further motifs along one long edge of the strip until you have two strips joined together. Keep adding motifs until you have joined the required number of strips together.

Chain spaces

Long strands of chain stitches, described as chain spaces, chain loops or chain arches, are an integral part of lace motif patterns. They are sometimes used as a foundation for stitches worked in the following round, or they may form a visible part of the design.

Changing the hook position

Working in slip stitch (see page 21) across one or more stitches is a useful way of changing the position of the yarn and hook on a round. Pattern directions may refer to this technique as "slip stitch across" or "slip stitch into". Here, slip stitches are being worked into the edge of a petal in order to move the hook and yarn from the valley between two petals to the tip of one petal, ready to work the next sequence of stitches.

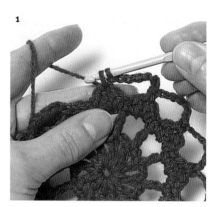

1 Work chain spaces as evenly as possible, anchoring them by working a slip stitch or double crochet into the previous round.

2 When a chain space is worked as a foundation on one row, stitches are worked over the chains on the following row. To do this, simply insert the hook into the space below the strand of chain stitches to work each stitch, not directly into individual chain stitches.

Lace motifs are very effective when joined together to make garments such as the Cobweb shrug (pages 86–7).

Joining lace motifs

Lace motifs are usually joined together on the final pattern round
as you work, eliminating the need for sewing.

1

1 Complete the first motif. Work the second motif up to the last round, then work the first side of the last round, ending at the specified point where the first join will be made, in this case halfway along a chain space at the corner of the motif.

2

2 Place the first and second motifs' wrong sides together, ready to work the next side of the second motif. Join the chain spaces with a double crochet stitch, then complete the chain space on the second motif. Continue along the same side of the second motif, joining chain spaces together with double crochet stitches.

3

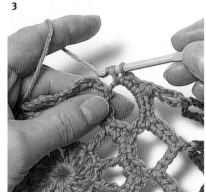

3 After all the chain spaces along one side are joined, complete the second motif in the usual way. Work additional motifs in the same way, joining the required number together to make a strip.

4

4 Work the first motif of the second strip, stopping when you have reached the joining point. Place against the side of the top motif in the first strip (wrong sides together) and join the chain spaces as before. When you reach the point where three corner chain spaces meet, work the double crochet into the stitch joining the two existing motifs.

5

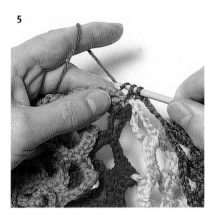

5 Work the second motif of the second strip, stopping when you have reached the joining point. Place against the side of the first motif in the second strip (wrong sides together) and join the chain spaces as before. When you reach the point where all four corner chain spaces meet, work the double crochet into the stitch joining the first two motifs.

6

6 Now join the next side of the motif to the adjacent side of the first strip, working double crochet stitches into chain spaces as before. Complete the remaining sides of the motif. Continue working in the same way until you have made and joined the required number of motifs.

Understanding patterns

Crochet pattern instructions are laid out in a logical sequence, although at first sight the terminology can look complicated. The most important thing is to check that you start off with the correct number of stitches in the foundation row or ring, and then work through the instructions row by row exactly as stated. All of the patterns in this book use written instructions rather than charts.

This pashmina (pages 44–45) may look complex, but the pattern is short and easy to learn.

Crochet abbreviations

The abbreviations used in this book are:

bch – beaded chain

bdc – beaded double crochet

C2 – yo twice, draw loop through stitch just worked, (yo, draw loop through first 2 loops on hook) twice, skip 2 stitches, yo twice, draw loop through next stitch, (yo, draw loop through first 2 loops on hook) twice, yo, draw loop through remaining 3 loops on hook

ch – chain

dc – double crochet

dec – decrease

dtr – double treble

exdc – extended double crochet

hdc – half double crochet

htr – half treble crochet

inc – increase

sl st – slip stitch

st(s) – stitch(es)

tr – treble or triple crochet

yo – yarn over

Essential information

All patterns provide a list containing the size of the finished item, the materials and hook size required, the tension of the piece and the abbreviations used in the instructions. Although many abbreviations are standardized, such as ch for chain and st for stitch, some of them vary, so always read the abbreviations before you start crocheting.

Repeats

When following the pattern instructions, you will find that some of them appear within curved parentheses and some are marked with an asterisk. Instructions that appear within parentheses are to be repeated. For example, (1 dc into next 3 sts, ch 2) 4 times means that you work the 3 double crochet stitches and the 2 chains in the sequence stated four times in all. Asterisks (*) indicate the point to which you should return when you reach the phrase "repeat from *". They may also mark whole sets of instructions that are to be repeated. For example, "repeat from * to **" means repeat the instructions between the single and double asterisks.

You may also find asterisks used in instructions that tell you how to work any stitches remaining after the last complete repeat of a stitch sequence is worked. For example, repeat from *, ending with 1 dc into each of last 2 sts, turn, means that you have two stitches left at the end of

TIP: TAKE NOTES

Each stitch pattern worked in rows is written using a specific number of pattern rows and the sequence is repeated until the crochet is the correct length. When working a complicated stitch pattern, always make a note of exactly which row you are working.

the row after working the last repeat. In this case, work one double crochet into each of the last two stitches before turning to begin the next row.

Additional information

You may find a number enclosed in parentheses at the end of a row or round. This indicates the total number of stitches to be worked in that particular row or round. For example, (12 spaced dc) at the end of a round means that you have to work 12 double crochet stitches in the round, each one spaced by the number of chains stated in the instructions.

Tension

The term tension refers to the number of stitches and rows contained in a given width and length of crochet fabric, usually 10 cm (4 in.) square. You will find that everybody has their own personal tension when working a crochet fabric. It varies from person to person, even when the same yarn and hook size are used. Crochet patterns are written using a specific tension in mind and, if your tension differs from the one given, the finished piece could come out either too big or too small. That is why it is important to check your tension before starting a pattern.

Making a test swatch

Using the recommended hook size and yarn, make a crochet piece approx 15–20 cm (6–8 in.) square, taking into account the number of stitches and rows in the stitch pattern. Fasten off and then block the sample (see pages 32–33). It is vital to work the tension sample in the exact pattern you will use for the main piece.

1 Lay the sample right side up on a flat surface. Using a ruler or tape measure, measure 10 cm (4 in.) horizontally across a row of stitches. Insert pins exactly 10 cm (4 in.) apart and count the number of stitches (including partial stitches) between the pins.

2 Turn the fabric on its side. Using a ruler or tape measure, measure 10 cm (4 in.) horizontally across the rows. Insert pins exactly 10 cm (4 in.) apart and count the number of rows (including partial rows) between the pins.

3 When working a stitch pattern, the tension may be quoted as a multiple of the pattern repeat rather than a number of stitches and rows. Work the tension sample in pattern, but count the number of pattern repeats between the pins.

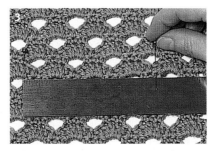

Adjusting your tension

If the number of stitches, rows, or pattern repeats to 10 cm (4 in.) match the pattern, you can get started. If you have too many stitches or rows or a smaller pattern repeat, your crochet is too tight – use a larger hook. If you have too few stitches or rows or a larger pattern repeat, your crochet is too loose – use a smaller hook. Block and measure the new tension sample as before. Repeat this process until your tension matches that given in the pattern.

TIP: HOOKS AND YARNS
Hooks and yarns from different manufacturers or in different materials can vary in size even if they are all branded the same. Always work a sample swatch to check that the pattern works for your materials.

How beads affect tension

Adding beads may slacken your tension slightly at the beginning if you have not used this technique before, as you can be so busy concentrating on placing the bead correctly that you forget about the tension!

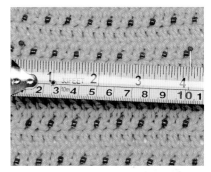

Using a bead that is bigger than your stitch will also affect your tension. Be prepared to experiment before finalizing your design if you are straying from a pattern. Until you are used to crocheting with beads, stick to the beads, yarn and tension as set out in the pattern.

Finishing techniques

A beautifully crocheted garment can easily be ruined by careless sewing up. Use a tapestry needle and a length of the yarn used to crochet the project, and select the method most suitable for the finished effect you want to achieve. Most crocheted fabrics need to be blocked before they are stitched together.

Fastening off

When your work is completed, you need to fasten off the yarn to stop it from unravelling. This is called fastening off or binding off.

1 Cut the yarn, leaving a length of about 10–15 cm (4–6 in.). Draw the loose end through the last loop on the hook.

2 Pull the yarn end to tighten and secure it.

Weaving in ends

After fastening off the yarn, you need to weave in all the loose ends. Thread the end through a blunt-ended needle with a large eye. Weave all the loose ends into the work, running them through the stitches nearest to the yarn end.

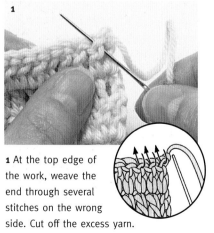

1 At the top edge of the work, weave the end through several stitches on the wrong side. Cut off the excess yarn.

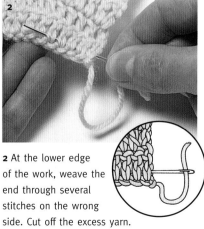

2 At the lower edge of the work, weave the end through several stitches on the wrong side. Cut off the excess yarn.

Blocking and pressing

When all the ends are woven in and before you start sewing the pieces together, you need to block and press them to the correct size and shape. To block crochet, pin the pieces onto a padded surface. Depending on the size of the piece you want to block, a variety of things can be used – ironing board, large pillow, a board covered with one or two layers of quilter's wadding or even the floor. Cover the padded surface with a check pattern cotton fabric. This will not only help when pinning straight edges, but also will withstand the heat of an iron. When choosing how to press the crochet pieces, refer to the information given on the ball band of the yarn.

1 Pin the pieces right side downward onto a padded surface using rustless glass-headed pins (plastic may melt) inserted at right angles to the edge of the crochet. Ease the crochet piece into shape, making sure that the stitches and rows are straight. Measure to check that each pinned out piece matches the finished size stated in the pattern.

2 For natural fibres such as wool or cotton, set the iron on a steam setting. Hold the iron approximately 2.5 cm (1 in.) above the fabric and allow the steam to penetrate for several seconds. Work in sections and avoid the iron touching the work. Lay flat and allow to dry before removing the pins.

3 Pin crochet pieces made from synthetic fibres as described in step 1. Do not use a dry or a steam iron. When heat is applied to synthetics, they lose their lustre and go very limp; in the worst cases you can melt the crochet and ruin your iron. When pinned out, spray the crochet fabric lightly with cold water until evenly moist but not soaked through. Lay flat and allow to dry before taking out the pins.

Seams

There are several methods for joining pieces of crochet together, including sewing the seams using a sewing needle or working a row of crochet stitches through the edges of the pieces using a crochet hook. It is really a matter of personal preference unless a pattern specifies a particular method. Use the one you are most comfortable with and that gives you the best finish. Seams are usually worked using the same yarn used for the main pieces, but a contrasting colour yarn can be used to make a decorative statement. A contrasting colour is used in these examples for clarity.

Overcast seam

Pieces of crochet can be joined by overcasting the seam. The overcasting stitches can be worked through just the back of the crochet loops or the whole loops. Place the pieces to be joined side by side on a flat surface with right sides facing up and edges together. Thread a large blunt-ended sewing needle with yarn.

1 Working from right to left, overcast the seam by inserting the needle into the back loop of corresponding stitches. For extra strength, you can work two stitches into the end loops.

2 Continue overcasting the seam, making sure you join only the back loops of the edges together, until you reach the end of the seam. Secure the yarn carefully at the beginning and end of the stitching.

3 Alternatively, overcast the two pieces together by inserting the needle through the whole loops of corresponding stitches. This gives a less neat join than sewing through just the back of the loops.

Backstitch seam

This creates a strong but non-elastic seam and is suitable where firmness is required and for light-weight yarns. With right sides facing each other, pin together the pieces to be joined. Insert the pins at right angles to the edge evenly across the fabric. Thread a large blunt-ended sewing needle with yarn.

1 Secure the end of the seam and yarn by taking the needle twice around the outer edges of the fabric, from back to front. Take the yarn around the outside edge once more, but this time insert the needle through the work from back to front no more than 1.3 cm (½ in.) from where the yarn last came out. Insert the needle from front to back at the point where the first stitch began, then bring the needle back through to the front, the same distance along the edge as before.

2 Work in backstitch from right to left along the whole seam, making sure that you stay close to the edge and go through both pieces of fabric. Secure the end with a couple of overlapping stitches.

Double crochet seam

Place the pieces to be joined right sides together. Using a crochet hook and working from right to left, work a row of double crochet stitches through both layers (see page 21).

Slip stitch seam

Joining pieces by slip stitching them together with a crochet hook makes a firm seam with an attractive ridge on the right side. Place the pieces wrong sides together and work a row of slip stitch through both layers (see page 21).

Woven seam

Place the pieces to be joined side by side on a flat surface, with wrong sides facing up and edges together. Thread a large blunt-ended sewing needle with yarn. Starting at the bottom and working from right to left, place the needle under the loop of the first stitch on both pieces and draw the yarn through. Move up one stitch and repeat this process going from left to right. Continue to zigzag loosely from edge to edge. Pull the yarn tight every 2.5 cm (1 in.) or so, allowing the edges to join together. A woven seam gives a flatter finish than a backstitch seam and works better when sewing together baby garments and fine work.

Edge finishes

Edge finishes can be worked directly
into the crochet fabric. Double crochet
edging is used mainly for finishing
necklines and borders on garments and
it can be worked in a contrasting colour
of yarn. Crab stitch edging is more
hard-wearing due to the small knots
of yarn made along the row. It can be
worked directly into the edge of a piece
of crochet fabric, as shown, or several
rows of double crochet can be worked
first to act as a foundation. Picot edgings
offer a more decorative finish.

Double crochet edging

Double crochet is a useful and flexible
edge finish. Working from right to left,
make a row of ordinary double crochet
stitches (see page 21) into the edge of the
crochet fabric, spacing the stitches evenly
along the edge.

Crab stitch edging

Also known as reverse treble crochet, this
stitch makes a strong, fairly rigid edging
with an attractive texture. Unlike most
other crochet techniques, this stitch is
worked from left to right along the row.

1 Keeping the yarn to the left, insert
the hook from front to back into the next
stitch and wrap the yarn over the hook.

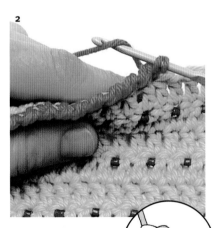

2 Draw the loop
through the stitch from
back to front so that
there are now two loops
on the hook. Finish by
wrapping the yarn over the hook again,
then draw the yarn through both loops to
complete the stitch.

Picot edging

This stitch makes a delicate edge
with tiny protruding loops of yarn. Work
a foundation row of double crochet
and then turn the work.

1 Work three chain stitches, then work
a slip stitch into the third chain from the
hook. This makes one picot.

2 Skip the next stitch, then work a slip
stitch into the following stitch. Repeat from
the beginning of step 1 and continue
doing so all along the edge.

Wearable Accessories

Project 1: Beaded ruffle scarf

This gloriously tactile spiral scarf is very easy to crochet and looks fabulous. It's a great way to practise your increasing technique. It is crocheted in two different weights, the lambswool-and-kid-mohair aran-weight yarn is edged with a lightweight cobweb kid-mohair-and-silk yarn with glass beads along the outer edge.

before you start

MATERIALS

Yarn A: 3 x 50 g (1.75 oz) balls aran-weight lambswool-and-kid-mohair blend (approximately 140 m/153 yds per ball) in red
Yarn B: 1 x 25 g (0.9 oz) ball laceweight 2-ply kid-mohair-and-silk blend (approximately 210 m/ 230 yds per ball) in deep red
Approximately 110 multicoloured large glass beads

HOOK SIZE

UK 4 (6.0 mm)

TENSION

Not applicable for this project.

FINISHED SIZE

Approximately 190 cm (74 in.) long and 11 cm (4.5 in.) wide.

ABBREVIATIONS

bdc – beaded double crochet
beg – beginning
ch – chain
dc – double crochet
dtr – double treble
rnd – round
sp – space
ss – slip stitch
st(s) – stitch(es)
yo – yarn over

SCARF PATTERN

Using yarn A, ch 161.

Rnd 1: Dc into second ch from the hook and into each ch, working 2 dc into last ch st. Working in remaining loops of beginning chain already worked, dc into each ch across, working 2 dc into the last ch st. Join with sl st to first dc of rnd.
Rnd 2: Ch 3, work 2 dtr into every dc. Join with sl st into top of beg ch 3.

Rnd 3: Ch 3, work 3 dtr into each of the next 320 sts (first half of round). Finish off yarn A. Do not turn. Thread beads onto yarn B. Join yarn B with a slip stitch to base of last dtr worked. Working in the remaining sts of rnd 2, bdc into next dtr, *dc in next 2 sts, bdc in next st, repeat from * across, ending with sl st to base of beginning dtr of rnd.

Break off yarn and weave in ends.

Project 2: Lace-effect shawl

Wrap yourself up in this luxurious shawl. Each square is worked separately using combinations of a DK tweed wool in a soft green and a variety of tonal shades in a 2-ply kid-mohair-and-silk blend. This creates a wonderful colour change throughout. The squares are simply crocheted together with the cobweb 2-ply and beads placed throughout.

before you start

MATERIALS

Yarn A: 5 skeins DK-weight merino wool, alpaca, viscose mix (approximately 175 m/192 yds per 50 g/1.75 oz ball) in olive green
Yarn B: 1 skein worsted-weight kid-mohair-and-silk blend (approximately 210 m/230 yds per 50 g/1.75 oz ball) in pale blue
Yarn C: 1 skein worsted-weight kid-mohair-and-silk-blend (approximately 210 m/230 yds per 50 g/1.75 oz ball) in green
Yarn D: 1 skein worsted-weight kid-mohair-and-silk blend (approximately 210 m/230 yds per 50 g/1.75 oz ball) in black
500 silver-lined, clear glass beads

HOOK SIZE

UK 7 (4.0 mm)

TENSION

10 cm (4 in.) per motif

FINISHED SIZE

122 cm (48 in.) by 40 cm (16 in.)

ABBREVIATIONS

bdc – beaded double crochet
beg – beginning
ch – chain
dc – double crochet
lp – loop
sl st – slip stitch
sp – space
tr – treble crochet
ws – wrong side

MOTIF

Make 24 motifs with yarns A and B held together, 12 motifs with yarns A and C held together, and 12 motifs with yarns A and D held together.
Ch 6, join to form a ring.

Rnd 1: Ch 6 (counts as tr plus 3 ch), *3 tr into ring, ch 1, rep from * twice more, 2 tr into ring, join with sl st into third ch of beg ch 6.

Rnd 2: Sl st into next ch sp, ch 6, 3 tr into same sp, *ch 1, (3 tr, ch 3, 3 tr) into next ch sp, rep from * twice more, 2 tr into next ch sp, join with sl st into third ch of beg ch 6.

Rnd 3: Sl st into next ch sp, ch 6, 3 tr into same sp, *ch 1, 3 tr into next sp, ch 1, (3 tr, ch 3, 3 tr into corner sp, rep from * twice more, ch 1, 3 tr into next sp, ch 1, 2 tr into next space, join with sl st into third ch of beg ch 6.
Fasten off.

JOINING

Thread beads onto yarn B. Join motifs according to the diagram below.

Hold motifs with ws together and yarn B motif facing you. Join yarn A with sl st in upper right corner lp of yarn B motif. Bdc in same lp, ch 1. Bdc in corresponding corner lp of yarn C motif behind. *Ch 1, bdc in next ch lp of yarn B motif, ch 1, bdc in next ch lp of yarn C motif. Rep from * until upper left corner of yarn C motif has been worked. Fasten off.

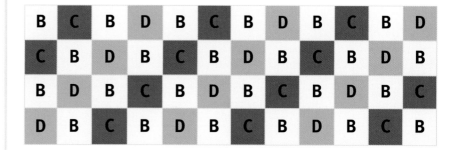

New skills/Joining squares together

When you have lots of squares to join, it is best to work in sections. Join individual squares to make strips, and then join these strips together. Zig-zag from one square to the next using a mixture of chains and beaded double crochet techniques.

1 Thread all beads onto yarn in sequence. Hold squares with right sides outside. Join yarn at top upper right hand corner of front square and work 1 dc.

2 Work 1 bdc into same place as dc, work 1 ch, then 1 bdc into top corner of square that is held to the back. Work 1 ch.

3 Work 1 bdc into first sp from corner of front square, 1 ch, 1 bdc into top of centre double of back square. Rep steps 1 and 2, moving along 1 st/sp each time.

Project 3: Wrist warmers

These wrist warmers are a pretty yet practical piece, a fun and funky way to add your own touch to an outfit. Worked mainly in a kid-mohair-and-silk 2-ply yarn, they are soft, light and cosy. Try making them in vibrant contrasting colours. They are perfect for wearing with a jacket and jumper, keeping you warm, but letting you wriggle your fingers, while the beaded trim adds that finishing touch.

before you start

MATERIALS

Yarn A: laceweight kid-mohair-and-silk blend (approximately 100 m/109 yds per 25 g/0.8 oz) in green
Yarn B: 1 x 50 g (1.75 oz) ball sport-weight cotton (approximately 113 m/123 yds per ball) in teal
Approximately 200 small black beads

HOOK SIZE

UK 9 (3.5 mm)

TENSION

5 groups of crossed tr to 10 cm (4 in.)

FINISHED SIZE

20 cm (8 in.) diameter, 12.5 cm (5 in.) long

ABBREVIATIONS

bdc – beaded double crochet
ch – chain
dc – double crochet
rnd – round
rs – right side
sk – skip
tr – treble crochet
ws – wrong side

MITTEN

Make 2.

Row 1: Using yarn A, ch 44. Tr in third ch from hook. *Sk one ch, tr in next 3 ch, work tr in skipped ch to surround last 3 tr worked. Repeat from * across. Tr in last ch, turn (42 sts including turning ch).

Rows 2–7: Ch 2 (counts as first tr), *skip next tr, tr in next 3 sts, work tr in skipped st to surround last 3 tr worked. Repeat from * across. Tr in last tr, turn.

Break off yarn and sew in ends. Sew side seam, leaving a 3-cm (1.25-in.) opening for thumb.

EDGING

Rnd 1 (ws): Using yarn B and with wrong side of work facing, join with sl st in last row of mitten, at seam. Ch 1, bdc in each st around. Join with sl st to first bdc of rnd.

Rnd 2 (rs): Ch 1, dc in each st around. Join with sl st to first dc.

Rnd 3: Ch 1, bdc in each st around.

Finish off.

Project 4: Pashmina

This beautifully cosy, sumptuous pashmina is made with a comforting combination of a DK tweed yarn in a soft grey and a variety of tonal shades in a 2-ply kid-mohair-and-silk blend. The beads are placed throughout the stripe pattern to add an extra-special touch. It's a perfect accompaniment to any outfit—winter or summer!

STRIPE PATTERN

Using yarn A, ch 52.

Row 1: Tr into fourth ch from the hook, and into each of the next 2 ch. Work str as follows: yo, insert hook into last unworked st before the 3 tr group just made, yo, draw up a loop surrounding these sts so as not to crush the 3 tr group, [yo, draw through 2 loops] twice (str completed). *Skip 1 ch, tr in each of the next 3 ch, str, repeat from * 11 more times, ending with tr in the last st. Break off yarn A and begin with yarn B.

Row 2: Ch 2, turn. Tr into second tr of row, tr in each of the next 2 sts, bstr as follows: yo, bring bead up to hook, insert hook into last unworked st before the 3 tr group just made, yo, draw up a loop surrounding the 3 tr group as before, [yo, draw through 2 loops] twice (bstr completed). *Skip 1 tr from the previous row, tr in each of the next 3 sts, bstr, repeat from * 11 more times, ending with tr in the last st.

Row 3: As row 2. Break off yarn and begin with yarn A.

Row 4: Ch 2, turn. Tr into each of the next 3 sts, str * skip 1 st from the row below, tr in each of the next 3 sts, bstr, repeat from * 11 times, ending with tr in the last st. Break off yarn A and change to yarn C.

Rows 5–6: Work as rows 2–3.

Row 7: As row 4, changing to yarn B at end of row.

Rows 8–21: Repeat rows 2–7 twice more, then repeat rows 2–3 once.

before you start

MATERIALS

Yarn A: 3 x 50 g (1.75 oz) balls of aran-weight lambswool-and-kid-mohair blend (approximately 89 m/97 yds per ball) in grey

Yarn B: 1 x 25 g (0.8 oz) ball of laceweight 2-ply kid-mohair-and-silk blend (approximately 217 m/ 237 yds per ball) in rose

Yarn C: 1 x 25 g (0.8 oz) ball of laceweight 2-ply kid-mohair-and-silk blend (approximately 217 m/ 237 yds per ball) in blue

Approximately 340 purple glass beads

HOOK SIZE

UK 4 (6.0 mm)

TENSION

13 stitches and 4 rows to 10 cm (4 in.) over border stripe pattern

13 stitches and 5.5 rows to 10 cm (4 in.) over solid pattern

FINISHED SIZE

32 cm (12.5 in.) wide by 131 cm (51.5 in.) long

ABBREVIATIONS

bstr – beaded spike treble crochet

ch – chain

str – spike treble crochet

st(s) – stitches

tr – treble crochet

yo – yarn over

PREPARATION

Thread 192 beads onto yarn B and 144 beads onto yarn C

SOLID FABRIC PATTERN

Rows 22–53: Continuing with yarn A, ch 2, turn. Tr into each of the next 3 sts, str * skip 1 st from the row below, tr in each of the next 3 sts, bstr, repeat from * 11 times, ending with tr in the last st.

STRIPE PATTERN

Rows 54–74: Break off yarn A and change to yarn B. Repeat rows 2–7 three more times, then rows 2–4 once, ending by finishing off stripe border pattern: yarn A (without joining a new colour).

FINISHING

Draw all beads through to the right side of wrap. Weave in all loose ends and block to finished size.

Project 5: Beaded string bag

This design is a real blast from the past. The DK cotton and chunky wooden beads give that boho retro feel. The textural wooden beads stand out from the matte DK cotton, while the open mesh netting crochet stitch adds to the look. The simple drawstring loop handle can be easily extended so you can strap the bag across and go, perfect for fun at the beach or taking your shopping home from the shops.

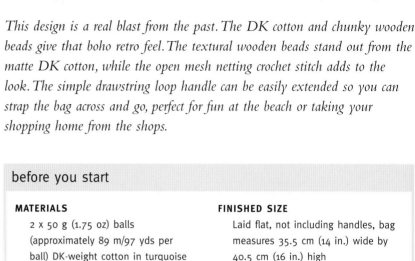

before you start

MATERIALS

2 x 50 g (1.75 oz) balls (approximately 89 m/97 yds per ball) DK-weight cotton in turquoise
127 pink 6-mm wooden beads
127 purple 8-mm wooden beads
127 natural 10-mm wooden beads

HOOK SIZE

UK 8 (4.0 mm)

TENSION

With chain loops fully stretched to form points, first round should measure approximately 7.5 cm (3 in.) diameter.

FINISHED SIZE

Laid flat, not including handles, bag measures 35.5 cm (14 in.) wide by 40.5 cm (16 in.) high

ABBREVIATIONS

bdc – beaded double crochet
ch – chain
dc – double crochet
hk – hook
lp(s) – loop(s)
rnd – round
sl st – slip stitch
tr – treble crochet

BAG PATTERN

Thread beads onto yarn in repeating sequence pink, purple, then natural. Approx 276 will complete the first ball of yarn.
Ch 8, join to farthest ch from hk with sl st to form a ring.

Rnd 1: Ch 1, work 1 dc into ring, *ch 9, dc 1 into ring, rep from * 20 more times. Sl st into first dc. (21 lps)
Rnd 2: Sl st into first 4 ch of ch-9 lp, ch 1, *bdc into lp as follows: bring bead up to

hook and work dc as normal (bdc completed), rep from * 20 more times, sl st into first dc to close round.
Rnds 3–19: Rep rnd 2 another 17 times. (Hint: the bag can be lengthened by adding reps of the final round, but remember that more beads would be needed.)

HANDLE

Ch 7.
Row 1: Tr into the third ch from hk and into each ch to end.

Row 2: Ch 2, tr into each st across.
Rows 3–80: Rep row 2.

FINISHING

Weave in all loose ends.
Thread strap in and out of ch lps of the last round of the bag.
Making sure that the strap is not twisted, sew the ends of the strap together.

New skills/placing beads in sequence

When more than one colour or type of bead is being used in a project, you have to remember to thread them on in sequence. Most patterns will give you this information, but remember that the first bead on will be the last bead worked.

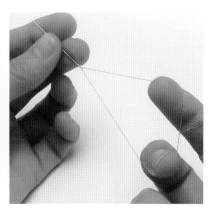

1 Thread sewing needle with sewing cotton thread and tie ends in a knot to form a loop.

2 Place beads in small tubs and lay out in front in sequence as indicated in pattern.

3 Place yarn being used through sewing cotton loop and begin threading on beads in sequence.

Project 6: Shoulder bag

This bag is very structured – the main body and handle are heavily felted to add a utility feel, while the sculptural shaping of the strap and the colour changes add to the effect. The crotcheted motifs, worked in a soft 2-ply kid-mohair-and-silk blend, soften the look and the beads add depth. The motifs look complicated, but are a simple twist on the picot mesh stitch.

BAG PANEL
Make 2.
Using yarn A and larger hook, ch 30.

Row 1: Tr in third ch from hook and in each ch across. Ch 2, turn.
Rows 2–8: Tr into each st across. Ch 2, turn.
Row 9: Tr into each st across. Change to yarn B. Ch 2, turn.
Row 10: Tr into each st across. Change to yarn A. Ch 2, turn.
Row 11: Repeat row 2.
Row 12: Repeat row 9.
Rows 13–14: Repeat row 2.
Row 15: Tr into each st across. Finish off and sew in yarn ends.

Make a second bag panel identical to the first.

With wrong sides facing, sew panels together along one side seam.

HANDLE
Open out newly joined seam.
With right sides facing, join yarn A with a sl st at top edge, 9 sts before the side seam.

Row 1: Ch 2, tr in each of the next 18 sts. Change to yarn B, ch 2, turn.
Row 2: Work tr decrease as follows: yo, insert hook into next st, yo and draw up a loop, yo and draw through 2 loops, (2 loops still on hook), yo, insert hook into next stitch, yo and draw up a loop, yo, draw through 2 loops, yo, and draw through remaining 3 loops. Tr decrease made. Tr in each of the next 14 sts, work tr decrease. Ch 2, turn.
Row 3: Tr decrease, tr in the next 12 sts, tr decrease. Change to yarn A, ch 2, turn.

before you start

MATERIALS
Yarn A: 2 x 100 g (3.5 oz) balls bulky weight yarn in feltable 100% wool (not superwash) approximately 80 m/87.5 yds per ball) in smoky grey
Yarn B: 1 x 100 g (3.5 oz) ball bulky weight yarn in feltable 100% wool (not superwash) approximately 80 m/87.5 yds per ball) in black
Yarn C: 1 x 25 g (0.8 oz) ball kid-mohair-and-silk blend laceweight yarn (approximately 210 m/230 yds per ball) in lilac
Approximately 150 glass beads

HOOK SIZES
UK 0 (9.0 mm) and UK 9 (3.5 mm)

TENSION
Not critical since project is felted, but not tighter than 8 sts per 10 cm (4 in.)

FINISHED SIZE AFTER FELTING
Body of bag measures 32 cm (12.5 in.) by 24 cm (9.5 in.)
Total length including handle measures 58.5 cm (23 in.)

ABBREVIATIONS
bch – beaded chain
bp – beaded picot
ch – chain
dc – double crochet
sl st – slip stitch
st(s) – stitch(es)
tr – treble crochet
yo – yarn over

Row 4: Tr decrease, tr in the next 10 sts, tr decrease. Change to yarn B, ch 2, turn.
Row 5: Tr decrease, tr in the next 9 sts, tr decrease. Ch 2, turn.
Rows 6–8: Tr in each st across. Ch 2, turn.
Row 9: Tr decrease, tr in the next 7 sts, tr decrease. Ch 2, turn.
Rows 10–25: Tr in each st across. Ch 2, turn.
Row 26: Work 2 tr into the first st, tr into each of the next 7 sts, 2 tr into last st. Ch 2, turn.
Row 27: Work 2 tr into the first st, tr into each of the next 9 sts, 2 tr into the last st. Finish off and sew in ends.

ASSEMBLY
Turn bag with right sides together and sew remaining side seam.
Stitch end of handle into place.

FELTING INSTRUCTIONS
Place bag in washing machine along with an old pair of blue jeans or other sturdy fabric. Avoid towels as these can leave fibres on your bag. Wash in warm water (detergent optional), agitating until bag shrinks to finished size. Note that this may take more than one wash cycle. Once bag is felted to finished size, lay flat to dry.

Shoulder bag motifs

MOTIF 1

Make 2.

Thread 6 beads onto yarn.

Using yarn C and smaller hook, ch 20.

Row 1: Dc into eighth ch from hook, make beaded picot (bp) as follows: ch 1, bch, ch, sl st into base of dc just made. Beaded picot made. *Ch 5, skip 3 ch, bp, repeat from * 2 more times. Turn to work next row into foundation chain.

Row 2: *Ch 5, dc into ch 3 space, bp, repeat from * once more.

Fasten off.

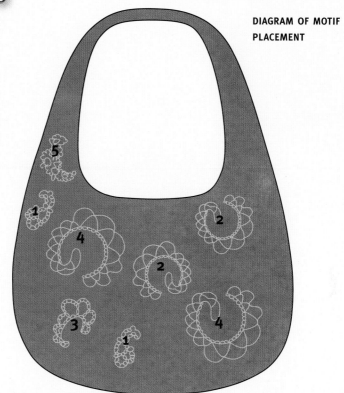

MOTIF 2

Make 2.

Thread 26 beads onto yarn. Using yarn C and smaller hook bch, (ch 3, bc) 9 times, ch 4.

Row 1: Dc into eighth ch from hook, bp, (ch 7, skip 3 ch, dc, bp) 5 times, (ch 5, skip 3 ch, dc, bp) 3 times. Turn.

Row 2: (Ch 5, dc into ch space, bp) 5 times. Turn.

Row 3: (Ch 5, dc into ch space, bpc) twice.

Fasten off.

MOTIF 3

Make 1.

Thread 14 beads onto yarn. Using yarn C and smaller hook, bch, (ch 3, bc) 6 times, ch 4.

Row 1: Dc into eighth ch from hook, bp, ch 5, skip 3 ch, dc, bp, ch 7, skip 3 ch, dc, bp, ch 9, skip 3 ch, dc, bp, ch 7, skip 3 ch, dc, bp, ch 5, skip 3 ch, dc, bp, ch 3, skip 3 ch, dc, bp.

Fasten off.

MOTIF 4

Make 2.

Thread 27 beads onto yarn. Using yarn C and smaller hook bch, (ch 3, bc) 9 times, ch 4.

Row 1: Dc into eighth ch from hook, (ch 5, dc, bp, skip 3 ch) 5 times, (ch 7, dc, bp, skip 3 ch) 3 times, (ch 5, dc, bp, skip 3 ch) twice. Turn.

Row 2: (Ch 5, dc into next ch space, bp) 3 times, (ch 7, dc into next ch space, bp) 3 times.

Fasten off.

MOTIF 5

Make 1.

Thread 7 beads onto yarn. Using yarn C and smaller hook ch 24.

Row 1: Dc into eighth ch from hook, bp, (ch 5, dc, bp, skip 3 ch) twice, ch 7, dc, bp, skip 3 ch, ch 7, dc, bp. Turn.

Row 2: (Ch 7, dc into next ch space, bp) twice, ch 5, dc into ch space, bp.

Fasten off.

Project 7: Evening bag

This little bag is perfect for a night out on the town. The dark chocolate background sparkles with bright beads in a modern colour combination. Made out of two rectangles with a large slash for a handle, the all-over beaded fabric adds weight and body to the medium-weight cotton bag. It is a great project to do if you've just mastered the basics.

before you start

MATERIALS
2 x 50 g (1.75 oz) balls sport-weight cotton (approx 113 m/ 123 yds per ball) in brown
240 dark turquoise glass beads
280 green glass beads
220 silvery green glass beads

HOOK SIZE
UK 9 (3.5 mm)

TENSION
19 stiches and 24 rows over 10 cm (4 in.) in double crochet.

FINISHED SIZE
19 cm (7.5 in.) wide by 20 cm (7.75 in.) high

ABBREVIATIONS
ch – chain
bdc – beaded double crochet
dc – double crochet
sl st – slip stitch
st(s) – stitch(es)

FRONT PANEL
Thread beads onto yarn in sequence, repeating (40 green, 40 dark turquoise, 40 silvery green) 5 times, then 40 green, 40 dark turquoise, 40 green and 20 silvery green.
Ch 36.

Row 1 (right side): Dc into second ch from hook and in each ch to end (35 sts).
Ch 1, turn.

Row 2: Bdc into each st across. Ch 1, turn.
Row 3: Dc into each st across. Ch 1, turn.
Rows 4–33: Repeat rows 2 and 3 to form beaded stripe pattern.
Row 34: Repeat row 2.

Make slash handle
Row 35: Dc into each of the first 10 bdc, ch 15, skip 15 bdc of the previous row, dc into each of the last 10 sts of row. Ch 1, turn.
Row 36: Bdc into each of the first 10 dc of the previous row, bdc into each of the 15 ch sts, bdc into each of the last 10 dc. Ch 1, turn.
Row 37: Dc into each st across. Ch 1, turn.
Row 38: Bdc in each st across.
Rows 39–42: Repeat rows 37 and 38 twice.
Row 43: Repeat row 37.

Fasten off.

BACK PANEL
Ch 36.

Row 1 (right side): Dc into second ch from the hook and in each ch to end (35 sts).
Ch 1, turn.
Rows 2–34: Dc into each st across.

Make slash handle
Row 35: Dc into each of the first dc, ch 15, skip 15 dc of the previous row, dc into each of the last 10 sts of row. Ch 1, turn.
Row 36: Dc into each of the first 10 dc of the previous row, dc into each of the 15 ch, dc into each of the last 10 dc. Ch 1, turn.
Rows 37–42: Dc into each st across. Ch 1, turn.
Row 43: Dc into each st across. Finish off.

FINISHING
Weave all loose ends into fabric.
Block panels to finished size.
With wrong sides together, sew along side and bottom edges.

Project 8: Flower pin corsage

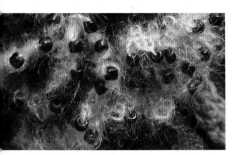

This pretty piece can be pinned onto anything; use it to jazz up a hat, jacket or bag. Delightfully feminine, the frilly kid-mohair-and-silk beaded petals almost froth and shimmer. Have fun creating your own colour combinations.

before you start

MATERIALS

Yarn A: 25 g (0.8 oz) ball sock-weight 100% wool (approximately 110 m/120 yds per ball) in green

Yarn B: 25 g (0.8 oz) ball sock-weight 100% wool (approximately 110 m/120 yds per ball) in purple

Yarn C: 25 g (0.8 oz) ball lacewight kid-mohair-and-silk blend (approximately 210 m/230 yds per ball) in grey

120 black glass beads

One pin backing

HOOK SIZE

UK 9 (3.5 mm)

TENSION

Round 1 laid flat measures 1.3 cm (0.5 in.) across.

FINISHED SIZE

13 cm (5 in.), by 9 cm (3.5 in.)

ABBREVIATIONS

bch – beaded chain

ch – chain

dc – double crochet

dtr – double treble crochet

lktrtr – linked triple treble crochet

rnd – round

sl st – slip stitch

tr – treble crochet

trtr – triple treble crochet

yo – yarn over

FLOWER PATTERN

Rnd 1: With yarn A, ch 3. Insert hook through second ch from hook, yo, draw up lp, insert hook in ring, yo and draw up a lp, complete tr as normal. *Insert hook down through horizontal lp around post of last tr made, yo, draw up lp, insert hook in ring, yo, draw up a lp and complete tr as normal. Rep from * a total of 5 times. Sl st to top of beginning ch 3 (6 sts).

Rnd 2: Ch 5. Insert hook through second ch from hook, yo, draw up lp, [insert hook in next ch, yo, draw up lp] twice (4 lps on hook). Insert hook in next st, yo, draw up lp. Complete trtr as normal. *Work lktrtr: insert hook down through uppermost of 3 horizontal lps around the post of last st made, yo, draw up lp. [Insert hook down through next horizontal lp, yo, and draw up lp] twice, insert hook in same st as before, yo, and draw up lp. Complete trtr as normal. Lktrtr made. Work 2 lktrtr in each st 5 times, join with sl st to top of ch 5 (12 sts).

Change to yarn B.

Rnd 3: Ch 1, Dc into each st around, join with sl st to first dc.

Rnd 4: Rep rnd 3.

Rnd 5: Ch 1, 2 dc into first st, 3 dc into each st around, ending dc into same st as first 2 dc of round, join with sl st to first dc of round (36 sts).

Rnd 6: Ch 3, (counts as first tr), 2 tr into first st, 3 tr into each st around, sl st into top of ch 3 (108 sts).

Fasten off yarn B.

Thread beads onto yarn C. With ws facing, join yarn C with sl st in any st of last round.

Rnd 7: Ch 1, dc into same st, * ch 2, bch, ch 2, dc into next st, rep from * around ending sl st into first dc of round (108 bch lps).

Fasten off yarn C.

STEM

Rejoin yarn A in ch base of first round of stem. Ch 20, dc into second ch from hook and into each ch across. Sl st into base of rnd 1 on opposite side of round.

Fasten off

Fold stem double and stitch sides together. Sew on pin backing.

New skills/working a linked triple treble

The linked triple treble stitch technique used in this project is essentially the same as a normal triple treble but is worked by going into the stem of the previous stitch or turning chain. In doing this we form a solid fabric but can still have the depth of the longer stitches. When working first linked triple treble, work into the turning chain.

1 Insert hook into uppermost of 3 horizontal lps around the stem of the last st made, yo and draw through.

2 Insert hook into the next horizontal loops around the stem of the last st made, yo and draw through, rep once more (4 lps on hook).

3 Insert hook into next st, yo and draw through. Yo and draw through first 2 lps, rep yo and drawing through 2 lps until 1 lp left on hook.

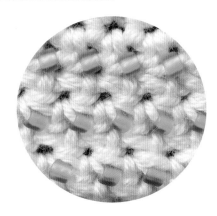

Project 9: Beaded beanie

This is a great project to practise your increasing techniques in the round. The rounded yarn adds something special to simple textures such as treble crochet. The beaded edge of the beanie is simple and effective; try threading on lots of differently coloured beads and see how the colours emerge.

before you start

MATERIALS
2 x 50 g (1.75 oz) balls 50% cotton, 50% wool, DK-weight yarn (approximately 113 m/123 yds per ball) in ecru
Approximately 300 matte green beads

HOOK SIZE
UK 9 (3.5 mm)

TENSION
17 sts and 14 rows to 10 cm (4 in.)

ABBREVIATIONS
bhtr – beaded half treble crochet
ch – chain
htr – half treble crochet
rnd – round
sl st – slip stitch
st(s) – stitch(es)
ws – wrong side

PATTERN
Ch 4, sl st in farthest ch from hook to form a ring.

Rnd 1: Ch 2, make 8 htr into ring, sl st into first htr of rnd (8 sts).

Rnd 2: Ch 2, work 2 htr into each st around, ending with sl st into first htr (16 sts).

Rnd 3: Ch 2, *2 htr into next st, 1 htr into next st, repeat from * around, ending with sl st into first htr (24 sts).

Rnd 4: Ch 2, *2 htr into next st, htr into each of the next 2 sts, repeat from *, ending with sl st into first htr (32 sts).

Rnd 5: Ch 2, *2 htr into next st, htr into each of the next 3 sts, repeat from *, ending with sl st into first htr (40 sts).

Rnd 6: Ch 2, *2 htr into next st, htr into each of the next 4 sts, repeat from *, ending with sl st into first htr (48 sts).

Rnd 7: Ch 2, *2 htr into next st, htr into each of the next 5 sts, repeat from *, ending with sl st into first htr (56 sts).

Rnd 8: Ch 2, *2 htr into next st, htr into each of the next 6 sts, repeat from *, ending with sl st into first htr (64 sts).

Rnd 9: Ch 2, *2 htr into next st, htr into each of the next 7 sts, repeat from *, ending with sl st into first htr (72 sts).

Rnd 10: Ch 2, *2 htr into next st, htr into each of the next 8 sts, repeat from *, ending with sl st into first htr (80 sts).

Rnd 11: Ch 2, *2 htr into next st, htr into each of the next 9 sts, repeat from *, ending with sl st into first htr (88 sts).

Rnds 12–22: Ch 2, htr into each st around, ending with sl st into first htr.
At end of rnd 22, break off yarn.
Thread beads onto yarn. Turn work so ws is facing. Join with sl st in any st of rnd 22.

Rnd 23: Ch 2, bhtr into each st around, sl st into first st of rnd.

Rnd 24: Ch 2, htr into each st around, sl st into first st of rnd.

Rnds 25–28: Repeat rows 23 and 24 twice more. At end of rnd 28, break off yarn.

With rs of work facing, join with sl st into beginning ring of rnd 1 (at top of beanie).

Rnd 29: Ch 2, work 5 htr evenly around ring in spaces between sts of rnd 1, sl st to first htr of this rnd.

Rnd 30: Ch 2, work one bhtr into each st of previous rnd, pulling beads to front of work. Sl st into first bhtr to join.

Project 10: Twenties-inspired scarf

The beaded crochet loop trim on this scarf gives it a real 1920s-flapper feel. Crocheted and beaded in soft appealing greens, the lightweight kid-mohair-and-silk yarn used is soft and light to the touch and the beaded borders add the swing.

before you start

MATERIALS

2 x 25 g (0.8 oz) balls kid-mohair-and-silk blend laceweight 2-ply yarn (approximately 217 m/237 yds per ball) in soft green
Approximately 940 green glass beads

HOOK SIZE

UK 8 (4 mm)

TENSION

Approximately 9 beaded loops per 10 cm (4 in.) width
21 stitches and 8 rows to 10 cm (4 in.)

FINISHED SIZE

11 cm (4.25 in.) wide by 132 cm (52 in.) long
Note that weight of beaded fringe may cause scarf to stretch longer and narrower.

ABBREVIATIONS

btr – beaded treble crochet
ch – chain
htr – half treble crochet
lp – loop
lphtr – loop half treble crochet
rep – rep
sl st – slip stitch
st(s) – stitch(es)
tr – treble crochet
ws – wrong side
yo – yarn over

SCARF PANEL

Make two panels.
Thread 470 beads onto yarn.
Ch 23.
Loop fringe.

Row 1: Htr into third ch from hook and in each ch to end (21 sts).
Row 2: Ch 2, turn. Htr into first htr. *Make lphtr as follows – bring 10 beads up to the hook, yo, insert hook into next st and pull up a lp, yo and draw through all 3 lps on hook (lphtr completed). Htr in the next st. Rep from * 8 more times.
Row 3: Ch 2, turn. Htr into each htr across.
Row 4: Ch 2, turn. Htr into first htr, *htr into next st, lphtr, rep from * 8 more times. Htr in each of the last 2 sts.
Row 5–7: Rep rows 2–4.

MAIN SCARF FABRIC

Row 8: Ch 2, turn. Tr in each st across.
Row 9: Ch 2, turn. Tr in each of the next 2 sts. *Work btr as follows – slide bead up to crochet hook and work tr as normal (btr completed). Tr in each of the next 4 sts, btr in the next st, rep from * 3 more times, ending row with btr, 2 tr.

Thread beads onto yarn C. With ws facing join yarn C with sl st in any st of last round.
Rnd 11: Ch 2, tr in each of the next 5 sts, *btr in the next st, tr in each of the next 4 sts, rep from * once more, btr in next st, tr in each of the last 4 sts.
Rnd 12: As row 8.
Rnd 13–60: Rep rows 9–12 another 12 times.

Next row: Htr in each st across.
For panel 1 only
Break off yarn at this point.
For panel 2 only
Row 61 (panel 2 only): Rep row 8
Row 62 (panel 2 only): Rep row 9.
Fasten off.

FINISHING

Sew all loose ends into fabric. Block to desired measurements.
Sew centre seam of scarf with a flat stitch.

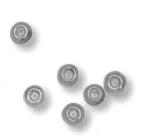

New skills/working a beaded crochet loop

This loop edge looks much more complicated than it actually is – whether you are placing 5 or 10 beads the same technique is used. The more beads you have, the longer the loop will be.

1 Work in pattern to required position. Bring the required amount of beads up to the crochet hook.

2 Insert hook into next stitch and complete as normal.

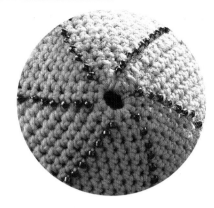

Project 11: Beaded beret

Crocheted in a woollen 4-ply rounded yarn, the increasing and decreasing techniques used to create the beret are used to place the beads throughout. The beads highlight the pattern – and watching the beaded spiral pattern emerge as you crochet is very satisfying!

before you start

MATERIALS

2 x 50 g (1.75 oz) ball sport-weight 100% wool (approximately 175 m/ 191 yds per ball) in pale blue
Approximately 250 glass beads in pewter

HOOK SIZE

UK 9 (3.5 mm)

TENSION

24 stitches and 27 rows to 10 cm (4 in.)

FINISHED SIZE

Approximately 24 cm (9.5 in.) diameter

ABBREVIATIONS

bdc – beaded double crochet
bdc dec – beaded double crochet decrease
ch – chain
dc – double crochet
lp(s) – loop(s)
rep – repeat
sl st – slip stitch
st(s) – stitch(es)
yo – yarn over

PATTERN

Ch 6, sl st in farthest ch from hook to form a ring.

Rnd 1: Ch 1, work 12 dc into ring, join with sl st into first dc (12 sts).

Rnd 2: Ch 1, bdc into the same st, *dc in the next st, (dc, bdc) into the next st, rep from * around, join with sl st into first st of rnd (18 sts and 6 beads).

Rnd 3: Ch 1, bdc into same st, *dc into each of the next 2 sts, (dc, bdc) into the next st, rep from * around, ending with dc in same st as beginning of rnd and sl st into first bdc (24 sts).

Rnd 4: Ch 1, bdc into same st, *dc into each of the next 3 sts, (dc, bdc) into the next st, rep from * around, ending with dc in same st as beginning of rnd and sl st into first bdc (30 sts).

Rnd 5: Ch 1, bdc into same st, *dc into each of the next 4 sts, (dc, bdc) into the next st, rep from * around, ending with dc in same st as beginning of rnd and sl st into first bdc (36 sts).

Rnd 6: Ch 1, bdc into same st, *dc into each of the next 5 sts, (dc, bdc) into the next st, rep from * around, ending with dc in same st as beginning of rnd and sl st into first bdc (42 sts).

Rnd 7: Ch 1, bdc into same st, *dc into each of the next 6 sts, (dc, bdc) into the next st, rep from * around, ending with dc in same st as beginning of rnd and sl st into first bdc (48 sts).

Rnd 8: Ch 1, bdc into same st, *dc into each of the next 7 sts, (dc, bdc) into the

next st, rep from * around, ending with dc in same st as beginning of rnd and sl st into first bdc (54 sts).

Rnd 9: Ch 1, bdc into same st, *dc into each of the next 8 sts, (dc, bdc) into the next st, rep from * around, ending with dc in same st as beginning of rnd and sl st into first bdc (60 sts).

Rnd 10: Ch 1, bdc into same st, *dc into each of the next 9 sts, (dc, bdc) into the next st, rep from * around, ending with dc in same st as beginning of rnd and sl st into first bdc (66 sts).

Rnd 11: Ch 1, bdc into same st, *dc into each of the next 10 sts, (dc, bdc) into the next st, rep from * around, ending with dc in same st as beginning of rnd and sl st into first bdc (72 sts).

Rnd 12: Ch 1, bdc into same st, *dc into

each of the next 11 sts, (dc, bdc) into the next st, rep from * around, ending with dc in same st as beginning of rnd and sl st into first bdc (78 sts).

Rnd 13: Ch 1, bdc into same st, *dc into each of the next 12 sts, (dc, bdc) into the next st, rep from * around, ending with dc in same st as beginning of rnd and sl st into first bdc (84 sts).

Rnd 14: Ch 1, bdc into same st, *dc into each of the next 13 sts, (dc, bdc) into the next st, rep from * around, ending with dc in same st as beginning of rnd and sl st into first bdc (90 sts).

Rnd 15: Ch 1, bdc into same st, *dc into each of the next 14 sts, (dc, bdc) into the next st, rep from * around, ending with dc in same st as beginning of rnd and sl st into first bdc (96 sts).

Rnd 16: Ch 1, bdc into same st, *dc into each of the next 15 sts, (dc, bdc) into the next st, rep from * around, ending with dc in same st as beginning of rnd and sl st into first bdc (102 sts).

Rnd 17: Ch 1, bdc into same st, *dc into each of the next 16 sts, (dc, bdc) into the next st, rep from * around, ending with dc in same st as beginning of rnd and sl st into first bdc (108 sts).

Rnd 18: Ch 1, bdc into same st, *dc into each of the next 17 sts, (dc, bdc) into the next st, rep from * around, ending with dc in same st as beginning of rnd and sl st into first bdc (114 sts).

Rnd 19: Ch 1, bdc into same st, *dc into each of the next 18 sts, (dc, bdc) into the next st, rep from * around, ending with dc in same st as beginning of rnd and sl st into first bdc (120 sts).

Rnd 20: Ch 1, bdc into same st, *dc into each of the next 19 sts, (dc, bdc) into the next st, rep from * around, ending with dc in same st as beginning of rnd and sl st into first bdc (126 sts).

Rnd 21: Ch 1, bdc into same st, *dc into each of the next 20 sts, (dc, bdc) into the next st, rep from * around, ending with dc in same st as beginning of rnd and sl st into first bdc (132 sts).

Rnd 22: Ch 1, bdc into same st, *dc into each of the next 21 sts, (dc, bdc) into the next st, rep from * around, ending with dc in same st as beginning of rnd and sl st into first bdc (138 sts).

Rnd 23: Ch 1, bdc into same st, *dc into each of the next 22 sts, (dc, bdc) into the next st, rep from * around, ending with dc in same st as beginning of rnd and sl st into first bdc (144 sts).

Rnd 24: Ch 1, bdc into the same st, *dc into each of the next 23 sts, bdc into the next st, rep from * around, ending with sl st into first bdc (144 sts).

Rnds 25–33: Rep rnd 24.

Rnd 34: Ch 1, *work bdc dec as follows: (insert hook in next st, yo and pull up a lp) twice, yo pull through all 3 lps on hook. Bdc dec made. Dc into each of next 22 sts, rep from * around. Join with sl st to first st (138 sts).

Rnd 35: Ch 1, *bdc dec once. Dc into each of next 21 sts, rep from * around. Join with sl st to first st (132 sts).

Rnd 36: Ch 1, *bdc dec once. Dc into each of next 20 sts, rep from * around. Join with sl st to first st (126 sts).

Rnd 37: Ch 1, *bdc dec once. Dc into each of next 19 sts, rep from * around. Join with sl st to first st (120 sts).

Rnd 38: Ch 1, *bdc dec once. Dc into each of next 18 sts, rep from * around. Join with sl st to first st (114 sts).

Rnd 39: Ch 1, *bdc dec once. Dc into each of next 17 sts, rep from * around. Join with sl st to first st (108 sts).

Rnd 40: Ch 1, *bdc dec once. Dc into each of next 16 sts, rep from * around. Join with sl st to first st (102 sts).

Rnd 41: Ch 1, *bdc dec once. Dc into each of next 15 sts, rep from * around. Join with sl st to first st (96 sts). At end of rnd 41, turn.

Rnds 42–45: Ch 1, dc in each st around. Join with a sl st to first dc of rnd. At end of rnd 45, fasten off yarn.

New skills/beaded increasing and decreasing in the round

Placing the beads where the increase and decrease happen makes a feature of the technique and also helps us remember where we have to increase or decrease. The technique is the same as normal, except we are placing a bead halfway through.

1 Work as normal to increase position.

2 Work first stitch of increase as normal, then place bead up at crochet hook, work double crochet into same place. Increase completed.

3 Work as normal to decrease position, then work first half of decrease as follows, insert hook into fabric, yo and draw lp back through towards yourself (2 lps on hook).

4 Bring bead up to hook and finish off decrease by inserting hook into next stitch, yo and draw lp through towards yourself, yo again and draw through all lps on hook.

Project 12: Textured beaded bag

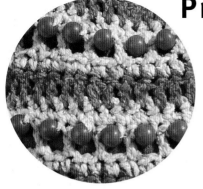

This bag is jam-packed full of different textures, colours and stitches, and is a great way to test your crochet skills. The raw finish of the silk-and-cotton blend aran-weight yarns enhance the textural stitches. The glossy wooden beads add a little bit of fun, giving the bag a sugar-candy appearance.

before you start

MATERIALS

Yarn A: 2 x 50 g ball (1.75 oz) worsted-weight cotton-and-silk blend (approximately 108 m/ 118 yds per skein) in pink
Yarn B: 1 x 50 g ball (1.75 oz) worsted-weight cotton-and-silk blend (approximately 108 m/ 118 yds per skein) in cerise
Approximately 150 pink 8-mm wooden beads

HOOK SIZES

UK 8 (4.0 mm) and UK 6 (5.0 mm)

TENSION

13 sts and 10.5 rows to 10 cm (4 in.) over beaded pattern

FINISHED SIZE

30 cm (12 in.) wide by 29 cm (11.5 in.) tall

ABBREVIATIONS

bch – beaded chain
bptr – back post treble crochet
ch – chain
dc – double crochet
fptr – front post treble crochet
sk – skip
sl st – slip stitch
st – stitch(es)
tr – treble crochet

BAG PANEL

Make 2.
Thread beads onto yarn A. Using yarn A and larger crochet hook, ch 38.

Row 1: Dc into second ch from hook and in each ch to end (37 dc). Ch 2, turn.
Row 2: Tr in each of the first 2 sts, * bch, sk one st, tr, repeat from * 16 more times, tr in the last st. Ch 1, turn.
Row 3: Dc into each dc and each ch space across (37 dc). Change to yarn B, ch 2, turn.
Row 4: Tr into each st across. Change to yarn A, ch 1, turn.
Row 5: Dc into each st across, ch 2, turn.
Rows 6–13: Repeat rows 2 to 5 twice more.
Rows 14–16: Repeat rows 2 to 4.
Row 17: Tr into each st across. Ch 2, turn.
Row 18–21: Tr in the first st. Alternate fptr, bptr across to form crochet rib pattern, ending tr into the turning chain.

HANDLE

Rows 22a–25a: Tr in the first st, *fptr, bptr, repeat from * 3 more times (9 tr in row), ch 2, turn. At end of row 25, skip final turning ch and finish off yarn.
Rows 22b–25b: Skipping 20 unworked sts from row 21, join with sl st in next tr. Ch 2, and work in fp/bp rib pattern for 4 rows to match right side. Do not break off yarn at end of row 25b. Instead, ch 20, skip unworked sts of row 21, and join with sl st in top of tr of row 25a. Sl st in remaining sts to end of row.
Row 26: Work first 9 sts of row, continuing in FP/BP rib pattern. Tr into each ch, and finish row in FP/BP rib pattern.
Rows 27–28: Tr in first st, *fptr, bptr, repeat from * across, ending tr in the last st. Finish off.

HANDLE TRIM

Using yarn B and smaller hook, join with sl st to bottom right hand corner of handle opening. Work 50 dc evenly around, joining in first dc of round with a sl st.

FINISHING OFF

Sew all loose ends into fabric. With wrong sides facing, stitch side and bottom seams together.

Project 13: Beaded necklace

This piece of jewellery is very simple to create, using basic increasing and decreasing techniques while working in the round. The ball and loop fastening at the back, the pewter beads worked into the joining chains and the shimmer of the 4-ply lurex yarn all give this necklace a special feel.

before you start

MATERIALS
25 g (0.8 oz) lurex (approximately 95 m/104 yds per ball)
Approximately 100 small pewter glass beads
Small amount of polyester fibrefill

HOOK SIZE
UK 2 (1.75 mm)

TENSION
Large bobble measures 3 cm (1.25 in.) in diameter

FINISHED SIZE
56 cm (22 in.) in length

ABBREVIATIONS
ch – chain
dc – double crochet
dec – decrease
lp(s) – loop(s)
rnd – round
sl st – slip stitch
st(s) – stitch(es)
yo – yarn over

LARGE BOBBLE
Make 1.

Ch 5, sl st in farthest ch from hook to form a ring.
Rnd 1: Ch 1, work 16 dc into ring. Sl st into first dc (16 sts).
Rnd 2: Ch 1, work 2 dc into each st, end with sl st into first dc of rnd (32 sts).
Rnds 3–6: Ch 1, dc into each st around, join with sl st into first st.
Rnds 7–8: Ch 1, work decrease (dec) as follows: (insert hook in next st, yo and draw up a lp) twice, yo, draw through all 3 lps on hook. Decrease made. Dec around, ending with sl st in first st (16 sts, then 8 sts). Finish off.

SMALL BOBBLE
Make 3.

Ch 5, sl st in farthest ch from hook to form a ring.
Rnd 1: Ch 1, work 12 dc into ring. Sl st into first dc (12 sts).
Rnd 2: Ch 1, work 2 dc into each st, end with sl st into first dc of rnd (24 sts).
Rnds 3–6: Ch 1, dc into each st around, join with sl st into first st.
Rnd 7: Ch 1, work decrease (dec) as follows: (insert hook in next st, yo and draw up a lp) twice, yo, draw through all 3 lps on hook. Decrease made. Dec around, ending with sl st in first st (12 sts). Finish off.

NECKLACE CHAIN
Thread all beads onto yarn. Ch 25, sl st in farthest ch from hook to make a ring.
Row 1: Ch 40,* bring 3 beads up to hook and work 1 ch as normal, ch 2, rep from * 11 more times. Sl st into top of first small bobble, ch 2, rep from * to * 12 times to match other side, ch 40, sl st into top of second small bobble. Break off.
Row 2: Rejoin yarn to top of large bobble with sl st. Ch 2, *bring 3 beads up to hook, ch 1 as normal, rep from * 4 more times. Sl st into bottom of third small bobble. Break off.
Row 3: Rejoin yarn to top of third small bobble with sl st. Ch 2, *bring 3 beads up to hook, ch 1 as normal, rep from * twice more and sl st into bottom of second small bobble (at centre front of necklace). Finish off yarn.

New skills/inserting stuffing

To help the crochet ball keep its shape, it is best to insert some stuffing into the centre before sewing up the opening at the top.

1 With the flat end of the crochet hook, poke a small amount of stuffing into the top opening of the ball. Keep doing this until the ball is quite firm.

2 Using the end of yarn at top opening (or if sewn in attach another piece of the yarn), darn it in and out around the stitches at top opening.

3 Pull together to close the opening and sew in loose ends.

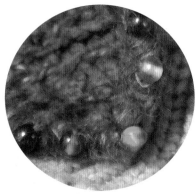

Project 14: Earflap hat

This hat can be worn in a variety of ways, so it's perfect for those changeable days. Worked on the round using a chunky tweedy yarn, the hat is given a bit of a twist with the woven-effect textured border.

PATTERN

Using yarn A and larger hook, ch 4 and join together with a slip stitch to form a ring.

Rnd 1: Ch 1, 15 dc into ring. Join with sl st to first dc.

Rnd 2: Ch 1, (dc into next 2 dc, 2 dc into next dc) 5 times. Join with sl st to first dc (20 sts).

Rnd 3: Ch 1, (dc into next 3 dc, 2 dc into next dc) 5 times. Join with sl st to first dc (25 sts).

Rnd 4: Ch 1, (dc into next 4 dc, 2 dc into next dc) 5 times. Join with sl st to first dc (30 sts).

Rnd 5: Ch 1, dc into each st around. Join with sl st to first dc.

Rnd 6: Ch 1, (dc into next 5 dc, 2 dc into next dc) 5 times. Join with sl st to first dc (35 sts).

Rnds 7 and 8: Repeat rnd 5.

Rnd 9: Ch 1, (dc into next 6 dc, 2 dc into next dc) 5 times. Join with sl st to first dc (40 sts).

Rnds 10–14: Repeat rnd 5.

Rnds 15–21: Ch 1, dc into back loop only of each st around. Join with sl st to first dc. Break off yarn.

EARFLAPS

Using larger hook and yarn A, with wrong side of work facing, join with sl st 6 stitches from back seam.

Row 1: Ch 1, dc into front loop only of next 9 sts, turn.

Row 2: Ch 1, dc into back loop only of next 9 sts, turn.

before you start

MATERIALS

Yarn A: worsted-weight 100% wool (approximately 100 m/109 yds per 100 g/3.5 oz) in brown
Yarn B: aceweight kid-mohair-and-silk blend (approximately 205 m/225 yds per 25 g/0.8 oz) in lime
Yarn C: laceweight kid-mohair-and-silk blend (approximately 205 m/225 yds per 25 g/0.8 oz) in brown
Yarn D: laceweight kid-mohair-and-silk blend (approximately 205 m/225 yds per 25 g/0.8 oz) in turquoise
Yarn E: laceweight kid-mohair-and-silk blend (approximately 205 m/225 yds per 25 g/0.8 oz) in mint
Yarn F: laceweight kid-mohair-and-silk blend (approximately 205 m/225 yds per 25 g/0.8 oz) in khaki
Approximately 60 multicoloured glass beads
2 large brown buttons

HOOK SIZE

UK 1 (8.0 mm) and UK 8 (4.0 mm)

TENSION

9 stitches and 11 rows per 10 cm (4 in.)

FINISHED SIZE

40 cm (15.75 in.) diameter, and 25 cm (10 in.) long

ABBREVIATIONS

bdc – beaded double crochet
beg – beginning
btr – beaded treble crochet
ch – chain
dc – double crochet
dec – decrease
sl st – slip stitch
st(s) – stitch(es)
yo – yarn over

Rows 3–10: Repeat earflap rows 1 and 2 four more times.

Row 11: Ch 1, working in front loops only, decrease (dec) as follows: *insert hook in front loop of next st and pull up a loop, repeat from * once, yo and pull through all 3 loops on hook. Dec made. Dc in front loops across to last 2 sts, work dec (7 sts).

Rows 12–13: Repeat earflap row 11. Break off yarn.

Skipping 11 sts on rnd 21 of hat, make second flap to match the first.

Sew in all loose ends.

TRIM

Using all kid-mohair-and-silk yarns together as one, thread beads onto yarn.

Using smaller hook and with wrong side facing, rejoin yarn at back seam.

Ch 1, bdc into first stitch at outer edge, (dc, btr) evenly around the outer edge of hat and around earflaps. Join with sl st to beg ch 1.

Sew buttons into position on hat and pin back flaps.

Project 15: Beaded head band

This is the perfect solution to those bad hair days. Working in a DK cotton using a small hook gives the head band its stretch and ease. The circular crochet units are quick and easy to make. Finish with a sprinkling of beads or sequins.

before you start

MATERIALS
DK-weight cotton (approx 89 m/ 97 yds per 50 g/1.75 oz) in ecru
Approximately 100 4-mm black beads

HOOK SIZE
UK 10 (3.25 mm)

TENSION
No real tension required

FINISHED SIZE
3.8 cm (1.5 in.) wide, 45 cm (18 in.) long unstretched

ABBREVIATIONS
ch – chain
dc – double crochet
dec – decrease
sl st – slip stitch
st(s) – stitch(es)
yo – yarn over

CIRCLES
Make 6.

Wrap the yarn approximately 10 times around 2 fingers on your left hand. Work a dc around the yarn to secure the ring. Work another 20–30 dc into the ring until you have filled the ring with sts. Sl st into the first dc of round. Fasten off.
Sew all six rings together to form a strip.

MAKING THE STRAP
Join with sl st to outer edge of ring opposite the rest of the strip.

Row 1: Work 5 dc along this edge, turn.
Row 2: Ch 1, dc into each dc across, turn (5 sts).

Row 3: Repeat row 2.
Row 4: Ch 1, decrease (dec) as follows: (insert hook in next st and pull up a loop) twice, yo, pull through all 3 lps on hook. Dec made. Dc once, dec over last 2 sts, turn (3 sts).
Row 5: Ch 1, dc in each of the 3 sts, turn.
Rows 6–25: Repeat row 5 another 20 times or until strap measures required length, keeping in mind that work will stretch in length.
Row 26: Ch 1, 2 dc into first st, dc into next stitch, 2 dc into last stitch, turn (5 sts).
Rows 27–29: Ch 1, dc in each of the 5 sts, turn.
Fasten off. Stitch into position at other side. Stitch beads into place along head band, according to photo.

Project 16: Brooch and pendant

These funky pieces are so easy to make; created from a simple crochet ball or loop, with beads sewn around the edges as decoration. The tweedy texture of the pure new wool 4-ply yarn used in the brooch, together with the mixed beads give the piece an organic feel. The pewter beads complement the shimmer of the 4-ply lurex yarn to make the necklace a special, sparkly little piece. Both pieces are so quick and easy to make that you'll soon be inspired to strike out and make your own design variants!

BROOCH

Ch 5, sl st in farthest ch from hook to form a ring.

Rnd 1: Ch 1, 9 dc into ring, sl st first dc (9 sts).
Rnd 2: Ch 1, 2 dc into each st around, sl st in first dc (18 sts).
Rnd 3: Ch 1, dc into each st, sl st in first dc.
Rnds 4–5: Repeat rnd 3.
Rnd 6: Ch 1, *decrease (dec) as follows: (insert hook in next st and pull up a loop) twice, yo, pull through all 3 loops on hook. Dec made. Repeat from * around. Sl st in first dec of round (9 sts).
Insert small amount of fibrefill into centre of brooch and run yarn around top of opening. Draw up yarn to close. Fasten off. Sew beads into position using picture as a guide. Stitch pin finding into position at back.

before you start

BROOCH MATERIALS
Worsted-weight 100% wool (approximately 110 m/120 yds per 25 g/0.8 oz) in natural
Nine 8-mm glass beads in various colours
Nine 4-mm glass beads in orange
Polyester fibrefill
Pin jewellery finding

HOOK SIZE
UK steel size 3 (1.25 mm)

FINISHED SIZE
4 cm (1.5 in.) diameter including beads

ABBREVIATIONS
ch – chain
dc – double crochet
dec – decrease
rnd – round
sl st – slip stitch
st(s) – stitch(es)
yo – yarn over

PENDANT MATERIALS
Sport-weight 100% wool (approximately 113 m/123 yds per 25 g/0.8 oz) in teal
Twelve 8-mm beads
Approximately 60 4-mm beads
Polyester fibrefill
Approximately one metre/yard of leather cording

HOOK SIZE
UK 14 (2.00 mm)

ABBREVIATIONS
ch – chain
dc – double crochet
sl st – slip stitch
st(s) – stitch(es)
tr – treble crochet

PENDANT

Make 2 sides.

Ch 15, join with a sl st in farthest ch from hook to form a ring.

Rnd 1: Ch 1, 18 dc into ring, join with sl st into first dc (18 sts).

Rnd 2: Ch 1, 2 dc into each st around, sl st into first dc (36 sts).

Rnd 3: Sl st into the first 9 sts, dc in next 3 sts, tr in next 5 sts. 2 tr into each of the next 2 sts, tr in next 5 sts, dc in next 3 sts, sl st into last 9 sts. Fasten off yarn.

Back stitch two discs together along outside edges. Stuff the disk with fibrefill and sew along inside edges. Sew beads onto bottom of pendant, using photo as guideline.

Use a lark's-head knot to loop cording through centre of pendant.

Garments

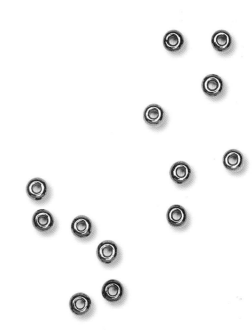

Project 17: Box crew-neck

This crochet edge-to-edge jacket is a great addition to your wardrobe. Worked in a DK-weight wool-and-cotton blend, the rounded appearance of the yarn brings a crispness to the stitch. This is a great way to progress onto garments and will help you understand how they are put together.

before you start

MATERIALS

Yarn A: 300 g (10.5 oz) DK-weight wool-and-cotton blend (approximately 113 m/124 yds per 50 g/1.75 oz) in lavender

Yarn B: 50 g (1.75 oz) sport-weight merino wool (approx 175 m/192 yds per 50 g/1.75 oz) in grey. Approximately 500 pewter grey 4-mm beads.

HOOK SIZE

UK 9 (3.5 mm)

TENSION

20 stitches and 9.5 rows to 10 cm (4 in.) over mesh pattern

FINISHED SIZE

45 cm (17.75 in.) long, 90 cm (36 in.) finished bust

ABBREVIATIONS

ch – chain
bch – beaded chain
bdc – beaded double crochet
dc – double crochet
rs – right side
sl st – slip stitch
sp(s) – space(s)
st(s) – stitch(es)
tr – treble crochet
ws – wrong side
yo – yarn over

BACK PANEL

Make 1.

Using yarn A, ch 91.

Row 1: Tr into third ch from hook and each ch to end (89 tr incl turning ch).

Row 2: Ch 2, tr into first 2 tr, *ch 1, skip 1 st, tr into next st. Repeat from * across. Tr in turning ch. Turn (44 ch sps).

Rows 3–21: Ch 2, tr into next tr and next ch sp, *ch 1, skip tr, tr into next ch sp, repeat from * ending with tr in turning ch. Turn.

Shape raglan as follows:

Rows 22–41: Sl st across the first 4 sts, ch 3 (counts as tr), tr in next ch sp. *Ch 1, skip tr, tr into next ch sp, repeat from *

ending with tr in turning ch. Turn. At end of row 41, you should have 43 sts remaining. Fasten off yarn.

FRONT PANEL

Make 2.

Using yarn A, ch 44.

Row 1: Repeat row 1 of back panel (20 ch sps).

Rows 2–21: Repeat rows 2–21 of back panel.

Shape raglan as follows:

Row 22: Sl st across the first 2 sts, ch 3 (counts as tr), tr in next ch sp. *Ch 1, skip tr, tr into next ch sp, repeat from * ending with tr in turning ch. Turn.

Row 23: Ch 2, tr into next tr and next ch sp, *ch 1, skip tr, tr into next ch sp, repeat from * until one mesh remains. Tr in last ch sp, tr in next tr. Skip remaining 2 sts of row. Turn.

Rows 24–33: Repeat rows 22 and 23 another 5 times.

Row 34: Repeat row 22 once more. Shape neck as follows:

Row 35: Ch 2, treble crochet decrease (tr dec) across next tr and ch sp as follows: (yo, insert hook in next st or sp, yo and pull up a loop, yo, pull through 2 loops) twice, yo, pull through all 3 loops on hook. Tr dec made. *Ch 1, skip tr, tr into next ch sp, repeat from * until one mesh remains. Tr in last ch sp, tr in next tr. Skip remaining 2 sts of row. Turn.

Row 36: Sl st across the first 2 sts, ch 3 (counts as tr), tr in next ch sp. *Ch 1, skip tr, tr into next ch sp, repeat from * until one ch sp remains. Tr dec across ch sp and next tr. Skip turning ch, turn.

Row 37: Repeat row 35.

Row 38: Repeat row 36.

Row 39: Repeat row 23.

Row 40: Repeat row 22.

Row 41: Repeat row 23.

SLEEVE
Make 2.
Using yarn A, ch 56.

Row 1: Tr into third ch from hook and each ch to end (54 tr).

Row 2: Ch 2, tr into first 2 tr, *ch 1, skip 1 st, tr into next st. Repeat from * across. Tr in turning ch. Turn (26 ch sps).

Row 3: Ch 2, tr into next tr and next ch sp, *ch 1, skip tr, tr into next ch sp, rep from * ending with tr in turning ch. Turn.

Row 4: Ch 2, tr into first 2 tr. *Ch 1, skip 1 st, tr into next st. Repeat from * across. Ch 1, work 2 tr in turning ch. Turn.

Rows 5–22: Repeat rows 3 and 4 another 9 times. At end of row 22, you should have 64 sts (31 ch sps).

Row 23: Sl st across the first 4 sts, ch 3 (counts as tr), tr in next ch sp. *Ch 1, skip tr, tr into next ch sp, repeat from * until two ch sps remain unworked. Skip rem. sts of row, turn (59 sts, 29 ch sps).

Row 24: Sl st across the first 2 sts, ch 3 (counts as tr), tr in next ch sp. *Ch 1, skip tr, tr into next ch sp, repeat from * until one ch sp remains unworked. Skip remaining sts of row, turn.

Rows 25–27: Repeat row 24.

Row 28: Sl st across the first 2 sts, ch 3 (counts as tr), tr in next ch sp. *Ch 1, skip tr, tr into next ch sp, rep from * across, turn. Repeat row 28 until 8 meshes remain. Finish off.

FINISHING

Sew shoulder seams, then set in sleeves. Sew side seams.

TRIM

Thread beads onto yarn B.

Rnd 1: With rs of work facing, work in unworked loops of front and back panels row 1 foundation chain. Join with sl st to bottom inside corner of left front. Ch 1, dc in each st along lower edge. Work 3 sts in the corner. Continue up side of front to neck edge. Work 3 dc in the corner. Continue working dc evenly along neck edge, placing 3 dc in each corner around entire garment. Sl st to first dc to join. Even though you are working in rounds, turn.

Rnd 2: Ch 1, dc in each st of previous round, working 3 sts into each corner until you reach the lower left front corner. Across the bottom edge of garment, make *5 bch, skip 2 dc, dc in the next st. Repeat from * across to end. Sl st into first dc of round 2.

SLEEVE TRIM

Thread beads onto yarn B.

Rnd 1: With ws facing, work in unworked loops of sleeve row 1 foundation chain. Join with sl st along side seam. Ch 1, dc in each st around. Join with sl st to first dc of rnd. Do not turn.

Rnd 2: Ch 1, *ch 5, skip 2 dc, dc in next st. Repeat from * around, ending sl st in first bdc of rnd. Fasten off.

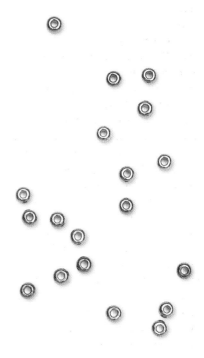

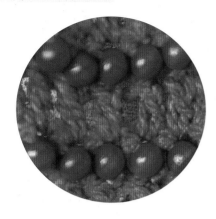

Project 18: Slash-neck top

This top looks far more complicated than it actually is. Worked in an open lace pattern, using an aran-weight cotton-and-silk blend, you will see results very quickly working through basic shaping techniques on the body. The beaded tie-belt feature is worked separately and then sewn on to the body.

before you start

MATERIALS

4 (5, 5) 50 g (1.75 oz) balls of cotton-and-silk blend (approximately 116 m/127 yds per hank) in red
Approximately 75 purple 6-mm beads

HOOK SIZE

UK 4 (6.0 mm)

TENSION

One 12-stitch pattern repeat and 6 rows to 9 cm (3.5 in.)

ABBREVIATIONS

bdc – beaded double crochet
ch – chain
dc – double crochet
dtr – double treble crochet
rs – right side
sl st – slip stitch
sp(s) – space(s)
st(s) – stitch(es)
tr – treble crochet
ws – wrong side

FINISHED SIZE

Small: 71 cm (28 in.) finished bust, 57 cm (22.5 in.) long
Medium: 89 cm (35 in.) finished bust, 66 cm (26 in.) long
Large: 107 cm (42 in.) finished bust, 75 cm (29.5 in.) long
Changes for each size S (M, L) are noted in parentheses.

PANEL

Make 2.

Ch 59 (62, 74).
Row 1: Dc into second ch from hook, (ch 5, skip 3 ch, dc in next ch) across. Ch 2, tr into last ch.
Row 2: Ch 1, dc into tr, skip ch 2 sp, * 7 tr into next ch 5 sp, dc into next ch 5 sp, ch 5, dc into next ch 5 sp, repeat from * across, ch 2, dtr into last dc. Turn.
Row 3: Ch 1, dc into dtr, *ch 5, dc into second tr of 7-tr group, ch 5, dc into sixth tr of same group, dc in next ch 5 sp, ** ch 5, dc into next ch 5 sp, repeat from * end repeat at **, ch 2, dtr into last dc. Turn.
Repeat rows 2 and 3 an additional 9 (11, 13) times, then row 2 once more.
Shape arm hole.
Row 23 (27, 31): Ch 1, tr into dc, ch 3, sl st into next 2 tr, ch 1, dc into second tr of 7-tr group, ch 5, dc into 6th tr of same group, dc in ch 5 sp, ch 5, dc in next ch 5 sp, *ch 5, dc into second tr of 7-tr group, ch 5, dc into 6th tr of same group, ch 5, dc into next ch 5 space, rep from * 2 (3, 4) times more. Ch 2, tr in last dc. Turn.

Row 24 (28, 32): Sl st into first 2 ch, sl st in dc, sl st in first 3 ch of ch 5 loop. Ch 3, 3 tr in same ch 5 loop, *dc into next ch 5 loop, ch 5, dc in next ch loop, 7 tr in next ch loop, dc in next loop, ch 5, repeat from * 1 (2, 3) times more, dc in next loop, 4 tr into last ch 5 loop. Turn.
Row 25 (29, 33): Ch 4, dc into third tr, *ch 5, dc into next ch loop, ch 5, dc into second tr of 7-tr group, ch 5, dc into 6th tr of same group, repeat from * 1 (2, 3) more times, ch 5, dc into second tr, ch 4, dc into turning ch. Turn.
Row 26 (30, 34): Ch 3, 3 tr in ch5 loop, *dc in next ch 5 loop, ch 5, dc in next ch loop, 7 tr in next ch loop, dc in next loop, ch 5, repeat from * across ending dc in next loop, 4 tr in last loop. Turn.
Repeat last 2 rows 5 (6, 7) more times.
Row 37 (43, 49): Ch 1, dc into first tr, ch 5, dc into ch 5 loop, ch 5, dc into fourth tr of 7-tr group, repeat from * across, ending ch 5, dc into last tr. Fasten off yarn.

BEADED TIE
Make 1.

Thread beads on yarn. Ch 8.
Row 1 (rs): Tr into third ch from hook and in each ch to end. Turn.
Row 2 (ws): Ch 1, * bdc across. Turn.
Row 3: Ch 2, dc into each st across. Turn.
Repeat Rows 2 and 3 another 4 times.
Work even in tr until strap measures approximately 123 (142, 166) cm or 48 (56, 64) in., ending ready to work a ws row.
Repeat Rows 2 and 3 another 5 times.
Final Row: Ch 2, tr in each st across.
Finish off.

ASSEMBLY
Sew body panels together along shoulder and side seams. Place marker at centre of beaded tie, and match to side seam. Stitch tie into position along bottom of garment.

Project 19: Halter-neck top

This fresh, feminine top is perfect for hot summer days. Simple and sophisticated, the detailing is all at the back and fastenings. The vertical beaded shell trims and crochet chains zig-zag across the back. Worked in medium-weight cotton, this top will keep you cool.

before you start

MATERIALS

5 (6, 7) 50 g (1.75 oz balls of sock weight cotton (approximately 113 m/124 yds per ball) in lilac
Approximately 300 purple beads
Approximately 300 blue beads

HOOK SIZE

UK 9 (3.5 mm)

TENSION

18 sts and 12 rows to 10 cm (4 in.)

TO FIT BUST SIZES

81 (91, 101) cm [32 (36, 40) in.]

ABBREVIATIONS

bdc – beaded double crochet
btr – beaded treble crochet
ch – chain
dc – double crochet
rs – right side
sl st – slip stitch
sp – space
st(s) – stitch(es)
tr – treble crochet
tr dec – treble crochet decrease
ws – wrong side
yo – yarn over

BODICE FRONT

Make 1. Note that instructions are written for smallest size, with changes in stitch count for sizes medium and large indicated in parentheses as follows: S (M, L). If only one st count is given, it applies to all sizes. Ch 78 (90, 102).

Row 1: Dc into second ch from hook and each ch to end, turn. 77 (89, 101) sts.

Row 2: Ch 3, tr in each st across, turn.

Rows 3 and 4: Repeat row 2.

Sizes M and L ONLY: Repeat row 2 one more time. Resume instructions at row 5 below.

Row 5: Ch 3 (counts as tr), treble crochet decrease (tr dec) as follows: (yo, insert hook into next st and pull up a loop, yo pull through 2 loops) twice, yo and draw through all 3 loops on hook. Tr dec made. Tr in each st across until 3 sts remain. Tr dec over next 2 sts, tr in last st, turn. [75 (87, 99) sts]

Row 6: Ch 3 (counts as tr), tr in each st across, turn.

Row 7: Repeat row 5 [73 (85, 97) sts].

Row 8: Repeat row 6.

Row 9: Repeat row 5 [71 (83, 95) sts].

Row 10: Repeat row 5 [69 (81, 93) sts].

Row 11: Repeat row 5 [67 (79, 91) sts].

Row 12: Repeat row 6.

Row 13: Repeat row 5 [65 (77, 89) sts].

Row 14: Repeat row 6.

Row 15: Repeat row 5 [63 (75, 87) sts].

Rows 16–17: Repeat row 6 twice.

Size M and L ONLY: Repeat row 6 a third time. Resume instructions at row 18 below.

Row 18: Ch 3, tr in the first st, 2 tr in the next st, tr in each st across until 2 sts remain, 2 tr in the next st, tr in the last st, turn [65 (77, 89) sts].

Row 19: Repeat row 6.

Row 20: Repeat row 18 [67 (79, 91) sts].

Row 21: Repeat row 6.

Row 22: Repeat row 18 [69 (81, 93) sts].

Row 23: Repeat row 6.

Row 24: Repeat row 18 [71 (83, 95) sts].

Row 25: Repeat row 6.

Row 26: Repeat row 18 [73 (85, 97) sts].

Row 27: Repeat row 6.

Row 28: Repeat row 18 [75 (87, 99) sts].

Row 29: Repeat row 6.

Row 30: Repeat row 18 [77 (89, 101) sts].

Sizes M and L ONLY: Repeat row 6 once. Resume instructions at row 31.

Row 31: Sl in first 8 (10, 12) sts of row. Ch 1, dc in next 61 (74, 87) sts, turn.

Row 32: Ch 3 (counts as first tr), 2 tr in each of the next 2 sts, tr across until 3 sts remain, 2 tr in each of the next 2 sts, tr in the last st, turn [65 (78, 91) sts].

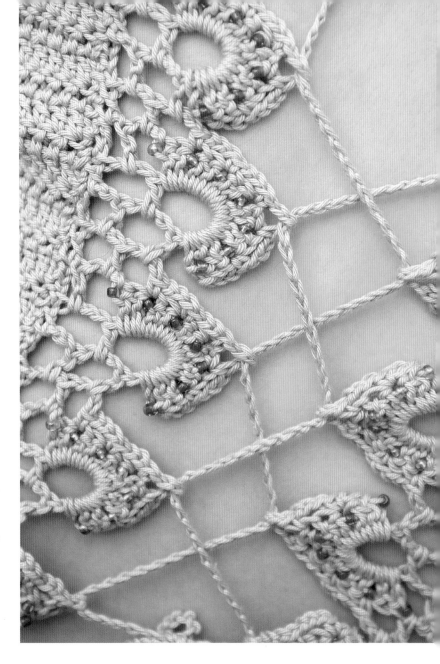

Rows 33–34: Repeat row 6 twice.

Rows 35–47 (49, 51): Repeat row 5 until 43 (52, 61) sts remain. Finish off.

BODICE BACK PANELS
Make 2.
Ch 29 (32, 35).

Row 1: Dc into second ch from hook and each ch to end, turn. 28 (31, 34) sts.

Row 2: Ch 3, tr in each st across, turn.

Rows 3 and 4: Repeat row 2.

Sizes M and L ONLY: Repeat row 2 one more time. Resume instructions at row 5.

Row 5: Ch 3 (counts as tr), tr dec. Tr in each st across, turn. [27 (30, 33) sts]

Row 6: Ch 3 (counts as tr), tr in each st across, turn.

Row 7: Repeat row 5 [26 (29, 32) sts].

Row 8: Repeat row 6.

Row 9: Repeat row 5 [25 (28, 31) sts].

Row 10: Repeat row 5 [24 (27, 30) sts].

Row 11: Repeat row 5 [23 (26, 29) sts].

Row 12: Repeat row 6.

Row 13: Repeat row 5 [22 (25, 28) sts].

Row 14: Repeat row 6.

Row 15: Repeat row 5 [21 (24, 27) sts].

Rows 16–17: Repeat row 6 twice.

Sizes M and L ONLY: Repeat row 6 a third time. Resume instructions at row 18 below.

Row 18: Ch 3, tr in the first st, 2 tr in the next st, tr in each st across, turn [22 (25, 28) sts].

Row 19: Repeat row 6.

Row 20: Repeat row 18 [23 (26, 29) sts].

Row 21: Repeat row 6.

Row 22: Repeat row 18 [24 (27, 30) sts].

Row 23: Repeat row 6.

Row 24: Repeat row 18 [25 (28, 31) sts].

Row 25: Repeat row 6.

Row 26: Repeat row 18 [26 (29, 32) sts].

Row 27: Repeat row 6.

Row 28: Repeat row 18 [27 (30, 33) sts].

Row 29: Repeat row 6.

Row 30: Repeat row 18 [28 (31, 34) sts].

Sizes M and L ONLY: Repeat row 6 once.

ALL SIZES: Fasten off.

BODICE CENTRE BACK PANELS

Make 2.

Thread beads onto yarn in the following sequence: *7 purple, 7 blue, repeat from *, until you have 79 (84, 84) beads threaded.

Row 1: Ch 11, tr in seventh ch from hook, ch 3, skip 3 ch, tr in last ch, turn.

Row 2: Ch 7, skip tr, tr in ch 3 sp, ch 3, skip tr, tr in ch 6 sp, turn.

Row 3: Ch 5, skip tr, tr in ch 3 sp, ch 3, skip tr, (btr, tr) 6 times in ch 7 sp, btr in same sp, turn.

Row 4: Ch 3, skip first btr and tr, (dc in next tr, ch 3, skip next tr) 5 times, dc into next tr, ch 3, tr in ch 3 sp, ch 3, tr in ch 5 sp, turn.

Row 5: Ch 5, skip first tr, tr in ch 3 sp, ch 3, tr in next ch 3 sp, turn.

Repeat rows 2 to 5 another 4 (5, 5) times. Fasten off

ASSEMBLY

Sew front bodice to side panels along side seams. Sew centre back panels to back bodice panels.

HALTER TOP EDGING

Thread remaining beads onto yarn, alternating purple and blue throughout. With ws facing, join with sl st at upper corner of back bodice panel. Ch 1, bdc in every st along straight edge. Then working up side of sloped edge, work 2 bdc around each tr, ending with one bdc in upper corner. Work a long chain for neck strap, skip sts along the upper row of bodice. Begin bdc again in next corner and work down sloped side, working 2 bdc in the end of each row, then bdc in each tr along top of remaining back bodice panel. Finish off.

DIAGRAM OF BEADED HALTER TOP

Body measurements sizes: small 32" bust • medium 36" bust • large 40" bust

1 square = 1 row or 1 stitch

4.5 sts/inch 3dc rows/inch

75 sts wide = 16.6"—33" finished bust (27" waist) • 37" finished bust (31" waist) • 41" finished bust (35" waist)

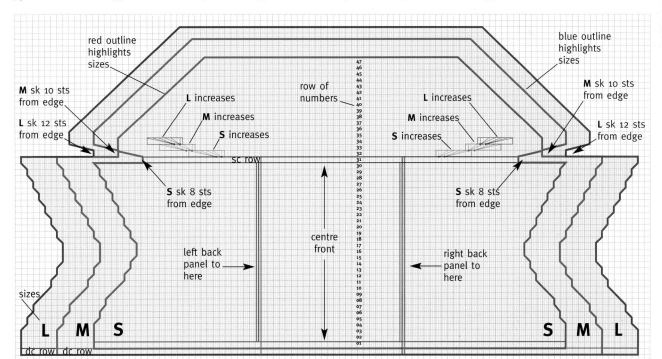

Project 20: Cobweb shrug

The shrug has become a new modern essential and can be found in lots of different shapes and sizes. In this design, each square is worked separately then stitched together to form the body and sleeves in one. The soft 2-ply yarn makes it ideal for summer evenings or layering up for winter nights. The beaded trim adds weight to the cobweb-light fabric.

before you start

MATERIALS
3 x 25 g (0.8 oz) laceweight kid-mohair-and-silk blend (approximately 210 m/230 yds per ball) in turquoise
Approximately 250 purple glass beads

HOOK SIZE
UK 9 (3.5 mm)

TENSION
Each motif 12 cm (5 in.) square

FINISHED SIZE
63 cm (25 in.) cuff to cuff and 38 cm (15 in.) long

ABBREVIATIONS
bdc – beaded double crochet
ch – chain
dc – double crochet
rep – repeat
rnd – round
sl st – slip stitch
sp(s) – space(s)
st(s) – stitch(es)
tr – treble crochet
ws – wrong side

MOTIF
Make 21.

Ch 10, join with sl st to form a ring.
Row 1: Ch 13, (work 5 tr into ring, ch 11) 3 times, 3 tr into ring, sl st to third ch of beginning ch 13.
Row 2: Sl st into each of the next 5 ch, ch 3 (counts as tr), (2 tr, ch 3, 3 tr) into same ch sp, * ch 9, (3 tr, ch 3, 3 tr) into next ch sp, rep from * twice more, ch 9, sl st to top of beginning ch 3.
Row 3: Ch 3 tr into each of next 2 tr, *(3 tr, ch 3, 3 tr) into 3 ch sp, tr into each of next 3 tr, ch 4, skip 4 ch, dc into next ch, ch 3, sl st into base of last dc worked, ch 4, tr into each of next 3 tr, rep from * around. Sl st to top of beginning ch 3.
Fasten off yarn.

ASSEMBLY
Step 1: Sew together motifs 1 to 17 according to diagram below, leaving open those edges marked with thick orange lines.
Step 2: Connect a single edge of motifs 1 and 12 along dotted line. You should now have a circular strip of 12 motifs with an additional 5 motifs extending from one side.
Step 3: Sew motifs 14, 15 and 16 to the now-continuous edge of motifs 12, 1 and 2, as marked with thick yellow lines.
Step 4: Sew gusset motifs 18, 19, 20 and 21 in place along edges marked with thick orange lines.

DIAGRAM OF SHRUG

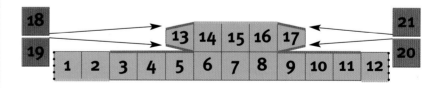

TRIM
Thread beads onto yarn. With ws facing, join with sl st along neck edge.
Rnd 1: Ch 1, dc into each st around the outer edge. Join with sl st into first ch.
Rnd 2: Ch 2, tr into each st around. Join with sl st into beginning ch 2.
Rnd 3: Ch 1, *dc in the next tr, bdc in the next tr, skip one tr, rep from * around. Join with sl st to first ch of rnd.

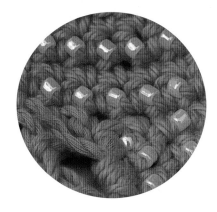

Project 21: Beaded tunic

Great for covering up at the beach or for throwing on over jeans. The chunky cotton yarn is worked in an open mesh fabric. The collar and front opening have a mandarin feel to them, edged with milky white pearlescent beads.

before you start

MATERIALS

Yarn A: twelve 50 g (1.75 oz) skeins worsted weight cotton (approximately 58 m/64 yds per ball) in pink

Yarn B: one 50 g (1.75 oz) skein DK-weight cotton (approximately 89 m/97 yds per ball) in pink

Approximately 400 white beads

HOOK SIZE

UK 2 (8.0 mm) and UK 7 (4.0 mm)

TENSION

13 stitches and 6 rows to 10 cm (4 in.)

FINISHED BUST SIZE

86 cm (34 in.), 58 cm (23 in.) in length

ABBREVIATIONS

bdc – beaded double crochet
beg – beginning
ch – chain
dc – double crochet
rem – remaining
rep – repeat
sl st – slip stitch
sp(s) – space(es)
st(s) – stitch(es)
tr – treble crochett

TUNIC BACK

With yarn A and larger hook, ch 64.

Row 1: Tr into third ch from hook and each ch across. Turn (62 tr).

Row 2: Ch 2, tr into first 2 tr, *ch 1, skip 1 st, tr into next st. Rep from * across. Tr in turning ch. Turn (29 ch sps).

Rows 3–23: Ch 2, tr into next tr and next ch sp, *ch 1, skip tr, tr into next ch sp, rep from * ending with tr in turning ch. Turn (29 ch sps).

Shape for armholes as follows:

Row 24: Ch 1, sl st across 8 sts, ch 2, tr in same tr and in next ch sp, *ch 1, skip tr, tr into next ch sp, rep from * until 10 sts rem unworked, tr in next tr and in next ch sp. Turn (48 sts, 22 ch sps).

Rows 25–34: Ch 2, tr in first 2 sts, *ch 1, skip tr, tr into next ch sp, rep from * until 2 sts rem, tr in each of the last 2 sts, turn. At end of row 34, finish off.

TUNIC FRONT

Work rows 1 to 21 as for tunic back.
Divide for upper front:

Rows 22A and 23A: Ch 2, 2 tr, (ch 1, tr in ch sp) 9 times. Tr in last tr, turn (22 sts, 9 ch sps).

Shape armholes:

Row 24A: Ch 1, sl st across 8 sts, ch 2, tr in same tr and in next ch sp, *ch 1, skip tr, tr into next ch sp, rep from * until 2 sts rem unworked, tr in each of the last 2 tr. Turn (14 sts, 5 ch sps).

Rows 25A–34A: Ch 2, 2 tr, tr into ch sp, *ch 1, skip tr, tr into next ch sp, rep from * until 2 sts rem. Tr in last 2 sts, turn. Finish off.

For upper-right front

Row 22B: With rs facing, in unworked sts of row 21, skip 4 ch sps from left front and join yarn A with sl st in next tr. Ch 2, tr in ch sp, (ch 1, tr in ch sp) 12 times. Tr in last 2 sts (27 sts, 12 ch sps).

Row 23B: Ch 2, tr into next 2 tr and next ch sp, *ch 1, skip tr, tr into next ch sp, rep from * across. Tr in last 2 sts. Turn.

Row 24B: Ch 2, tr in next tr, (ch 1, skip tr, tr in ch sp) 8 times, tr in next tr. Leave rem 8 sts of row unworked for armhole. Turn (18 sts, 8 ch sps).

Row 25B: Ch 2, tr in next tr and in ch sp, (ch 1, skip tr, tr in ch sp) 7 times, tr in last 2 sts. Turn.

Row 26B: Ch 2, tr in next tr, (ch 1, skip tr, tr in ch sp) 7 times, ch 1, skip tr, tr in each of the last 2 sts.

Rows 27B–34B: Rep rows 25B and 26B four more times.

Finish off.

ASSEMBLY

Weave in all ends. Sew front to back at shoulder seams. Sew sleeve seams. Sew side seams.

NECK TRIM

Thread approximately 75 beads onto yarn B.

Using smaller hook, with right side of work facing, join yarn B with sl st to bottom edge of neck opening.

Row 1: Work 34 dc evenly up right front edge to neckline. Turn.

Row 2: Ch 1, bdc into each dc. Turn.

Row 3: Ch 1, dc into each bdc. Turn.

Repeat rows 2 and 3 once more.

Break off yarn.

Repeat these 5 rows for left front edge, beg from upper left neckline and working 34 dc evenly down the left front opening.

COLLAR TRIM

Thread 150 beads onto yarn B.

Using yarn B and smaller hook, with right side of work facing, join yarn to right front at top edge of neck trim and work along the neck edge.

Row 1: Ch 1, dc into the end of each of the 5 neck trim rows, dc in each dc and in each ch sp around neck edge, 5 dc into left front neck trim.

Row 2: Ch 1, dc in the first st, bdc into each dc around until 1 st rem, dc in the last st. Turn.

Row 3: Ch 1, dc into each st across. Turn.

Repeat rows 2 and 3 once more.

Finish off.

Weave in all ends. Block to finished size.

SLEEVES

Make 2.

Using yarn A and larger hook, ch 42.

Row 1: Tr into third ch from hook and each ch across. Turn (40 tr).

Row 2: Ch 2, tr into first 2 tr, *ch 1, skip 1 st, tr into next st. Repeat from * across. Tr in turning ch. Turn (40 sts, 18 ch sps).

Row 3: Ch 2, tr in the same sp, (ch 1, skip next tr, tr in the ch sp) across until 2 sts rem, 2 tr into next tr, tr in the turning ch. Turn (42 sts).

Row 4: Ch 2, tr in the same st, tr in the next st, (ch 1, skip next tr, tr in the ch sp) across, ending tr in each of the last 2 sts. Turn.

Row 5: Repeat row 4.

Row 6: Ch 2, tr in the same st, tr in the next st, (ch 1, skip next tr, tr in next ch sp) across, ending with tr in next tr, 2 tr in the turning ch. Turn (44 sts).

Row 7: Ch 2, tr in next st and in ch sp, (ch 1, skip tr, tr in ch sp) across, ending tr in each of the last 2 tr. Turn.

Row 8: Repeat row 7.

Row 9: Repeat row 3 (46 sts).

Row 10: Repeat row 4.

Row 11: Repeat row 4.

Row 12: Repeat row 6 (48 sts).

Row 13: Repeat row 7.

Row 14: Repeat row 7.

Row 15: Repeat row 3 (50 sts).

Rows 16–21: Repeat row 4.

Finish off.

Project 22: Bikini top

This beaded bikini top is great for those hot sunny days. The turquoise glass beads scattered throughout almost seem to glow against the dark indigo background. The more you wear and wash this top the more it will fade, just like your jeans, and become a firm favourite.

before you start

MATERIALS

2 x 50 g (1.75 oz) DK-weight cotton (approximately 89 m/97 yds per ball) in dark indigo
Approximately 350 (425, 500) turquoise glass beads

HOOK SIZE

UK 9 (3.5 mm)

TENSION

18 sts and 10 rows to 10 cm (4 in.)

FINISHED SIZES

To fit cup sizes A (B, C). Linear bust measurement is adjustable to any fit.

ABBREVIATIONS

bdc – beaded double crochet
btc – beaded treble crochet
ch – chain
dc – double crochet
rep – repeat
rs – right side
sl st – slip stitch
st(s) – stitch(es)
tr – treble crochet
tr dec – treble crochet decrease
yo – yarn over

BIKINI CUP

Make 2.
Note that instructions are written for cup size A, with changes in stitch count for cup sizes B and C indicated in parentheses as follows: [A (B, C)]. If only one st count is given, it applies to all sizes.
Thread half of beads onto yarn. Ch 36 (42, 48).

Row 1: Dc into second ch from hook, *bdc in next ch, dc in next ch, rep from * to end, turn. [35 (41, 47) sts]
Row 2: Ch 4, (counts as first tr plus ch 1), *skip dc, tr in bdc, ch 1, rep from * across, turn. [17 (20, 23) spaces].
Row 3: Ch 1, dc in first tr, *bdc in ch sp, dc in tr, rep from * across, turn [35 (41, 47) sts].

91

Row 4: Ch 2, tr in first st, work tr decrease (tr dec) as follows: *yo, insert hook in st, yo, pull up a loop, yo, draw through 2 loops, rep from * once more, yo, draw through all 3 loops on hook. Tr dec made. Rep tr dec over next 2 sts, tr in each st across row until last 3 sts of row remain, while evenly distributing 7 beads across row. Tr dec, then tr in last st, turn. [31 (37, 43) sts]

Size B ONLY: Rep row 4 once more, distributing 8 beads across row. Resume from row 5 below.

Size C ONLY: Repeat row 4 twice more, distributing 8 beads across row on first rep and 7 beads on the second rep. [31 (33, 35) sts]. Resume from row 5 below.

Row 5: Ch 2, tr in the first st, tr dec, tr in each st across until last 3 sts of row remain, distributing 6 beads across row. Tr dec, tr in the last st [29 (31, 33) sts].

Size B ONLY: Rep row 5 once more, distributing 7 beads across row. Resume from row 6 below.

Size C ONLY: Rep row 5 twice more, distributing 7 beads across row on first rep and 8 beads on the second rep. [29 (29, 29) sts]. Resume from row 6 below.

Row 6: Ch 2, tr in the first st, tr dec, tr in each st across until 3 sts remain, distributing 7 beads across row. Tr dec, tr [27 sts].

Row 7: Ch 2, tr in the first st, tr dec, tr in each st across until 3 sts remain, distributing 6 beads across row. Tr dec, tr [25 sts].

Row 8: Ch 2, tr in the first st, tr dec, tr in each st across until 3 sts remain, distributing 5 beads across row. Tr dec, tr [23 sts].

Row 9: Ch 2, tr in the first st, tr dec, tr in each st across until 3 sts remain, distributing 4 beads across row. Tr dec, tr [21 sts].

Row 10: Ch 2, tr in the first st, tr dec, tr in each st across until 3 sts remain, distributing 5 beads across row. Tr dec, tr [19 sts].

Row 11: Ch 2, tr in the first st, tr dec, tr in each st across until 3 sts remain, distributing 4 beads across row. Tr dec, tr [17 sts].

Row 12: Ch 2, tr in the first st, tr dec, tr in each st across until 3 sts remain, distributing 3 beads across row. Tr dec, tr [15 sts].

Row 13: Ch 2, tr in the first st, tr dec, tr in each st across until 3 sts remain, distributing 2 beads across row. Tr dec, tr [13 sts].

Row 14: Ch 2, tr in the first st, tr dec, tr in each st across until 3 sts remain, distributing 3 beads across row. Tr dec, tr [11 sts].

Row 15: Ch 2, tr in the first st, tr dec, tr in each st across until 3 sts remain, distributing 2 beads across row. Tr dec, tr [9 sts].

Row 16: Ch 2, tr in the first st, tr dec, tr, btr, tr, tr dec, tr [7 sts].

Row 17: Ch 2, tr in the first st, tr dec, tr, tr dec, tr [5 sts].

Row 18: Ch 2, tr in the first st, (yo, insert hook in next st, yo and pull up loop, yo, pull through 2 loops on hook) three times, yo, and pull through all 4 loops on hook, tr in the last st [3 sts]. Finish off.

CUP BORDER

Thread beads onto yarn.

Row 1: With rs facing, join with sl st in lower right corner. (If working left-handed, join in lower left corner.) Ch 1, work approximately 60 dc evenly around 2 sides of cup, placing 3 dc in top corner, turn.

Row 2: Ch 1, bdc in first dc, *dc, bdc, rep from * across, working 3 sts in corner, turn.

Row 3: Ch 1, dc in each st, working 3 sts into corner, turn.

Row 4: Rep border row 2. Finish off.

NECK TIE

Join with sl st in corner st at top of cup border. *Ch 1, dc in next 2 sts, turn. Rep from * until tie measures 45 cm (18 in.) or desired length. Finish off.

Make second cup with border and neck tie identical to previous.

BODICE TIE

Make 1.

Ch 3, dc in second and farthest chs from hook. *ch 1, turn, dc in both sts, rep from * until tie measures approximately 120 cm (48 in.) or desired length. Finish off.

Thread bodice tie through eyelets created in cup rows 2.

ASSEMBLY

Wash finished bikini top in hot water to remove excess indigo dye. Lay flat to dry.

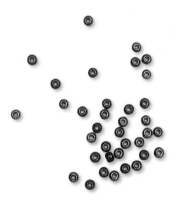

Project 23: Cap-sleeved wrap

Crocheted in a medium-weight 100% cotton yarn and worked in an open-mesh fabric with capped sleeves, this garment is light enough to fit under a jacket and is also great for wearing on its own on a summer day.

before you start

MATERIALS

300 g (10.5 oz) sport-weight cotton (approximately 113 m/124 yds per 50 g/1.75 oz) in beige
Approximately 300 pewter 4-mm beads
Approximately 300 orange 4-mm beads

HOOK SIZE

UK 8 (4.0 mm) and UK 10 (3.25 mm)

TENSION

22 sts and 9.5 rows to 10 cm (4 in.) across mesh pattern

FINISHED SIZE

43 cm (17.25 in.) long, 80 cm (32 in.) finished bust

ABBREVIATIONS

bch – beaded chain
bdc – beaded double crochet
btr – beaded treble crochet
ch – chain
dc – double crochet
lp(s) – loop(s)
rep – repeat
sl st – slip stitch
sp(s) – space(s)
st(s) – stitch(es)
tr – treble crochet
yo – yarn over

BACK PANEL

With larger hook, ch 84.

Row 1: Tr into third ch from hook and each ch across. Turn (82 tr).
Row 2: Ch 2, tr into first 2 tr, *ch 1, skip 1 st, tr into next st. Rep from * across. Tr in turning ch. Turn (39 ch sps).
Rows 3–26: Ch 2, tr into next tr and next ch sp, *ch 1, skip tr, tr into next ch sp, rep from * ending with tr in turning ch. Turn (39 ch sps).

Shape armholes as follows:

Row 27: Sl st into first 2 tr and ch sp, ch 2, tr in next tr and ch sp. *Ch 1, skip tr, tr into next ch sp, rep from * ending with tr in turning ch. Turn (37 ch sps).
Rows 28–43: Rep row 3. Fasten off.

FRONT PANEL

Make 2.

With larger hook, ch 62.

Row 1: Tr into third ch from hook and each ch across. Turn (60 tr).
Row 2: Ch 2, tr into first 2 tr, *ch 1, skip 1 st, tr into next st. Rep from * across. Tr in turning ch. Turn (28 ch sps).
Rows 3–9: Ch 2, tr into next tr and next ch sp, *ch 1, skip tr, tr into next ch sp, rep from * ending with tr in turning ch. Turn (28 ch sps).

Shape neck edge as follows:

Row 10: Ch 2, work treble crochet decrease (tr dec) as follows: (yo, insert hook in next st or sp, yo and pull up a lp, yo, pull through 2 lps) twice, yo, pull through all 3 lps on hook. Tr dec made. *Ch 1, skip tr, tr into next ch sp, rep from * ending with tr in turning ch. Turn (27 ch sps).
Row 11: Ch 2, tr into next tr and next ch sp, *ch 1, skip tr, tr into next ch sp, rep from * ending with tr in top of tr dec. Turn (27 ch sps).
Rows 12–25: Rep rows 10 and 11 another 8 times until 19 ch sps remain.
Row 26: Rep row 10 once more.
Shape armhole as follows:
Row 27: Sl st into first 2 tr and ch sp, ch 2, tr in next tr and ch sp. *Ch 1, skip tr, tr into next ch sp, rep from * ending with tr in turning ch. Turn (17 ch sps).
Rows 28–43: Rep rows 10 and 11 until 9 ch sps remain. Fasten off.

SLEEVE

Make 2.
Thread 68 pewter beads then 68 orange beads onto yarn. (The first bead threaded will be the last bead worked.)

Row 1: With larger hook, bch 68, then ch 2. Btr into third ch from hook (this is bch nearest to hook) and in each bch to end, turn (68 btr).

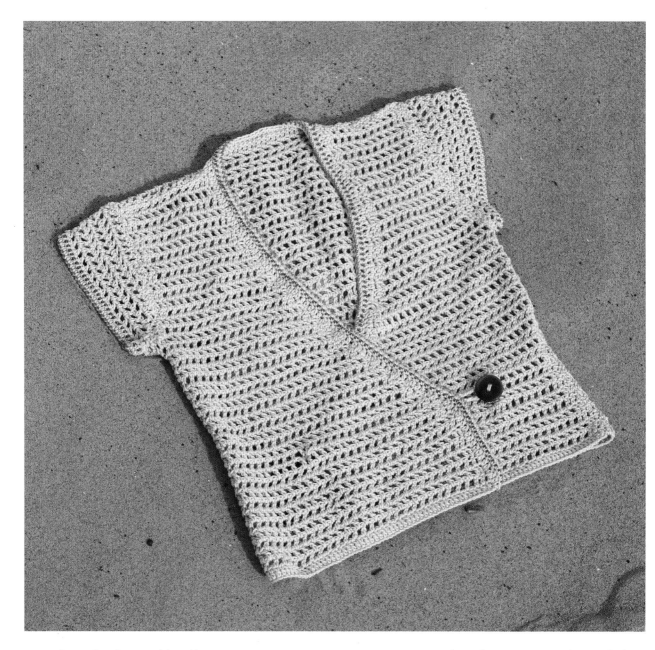

Row 2: Ch 2, tr into first 2 tr, *ch 1, skip 1 st, tr into next st. Rep from * across. Tr in turning ch. Turn (32 ch sps).

Row 3: Ch 1, sl st in first 4 sts, ch 2 (counts as tr), tr into next tr and next ch sp, *ch 1, skip tr, tr into next ch sp, rep from * across until 2 ch sps remain. Tr in next tr, sk remaining sts, turn (29 ch sps).

Rows 4–7: Rep row 3 until 17 ch sps remain. Fasten off yarn.

ASSEMBLY

Sew front panels to back at shoulder seams. Set in sleeves. Sew side seams.

TRIM

Thread 180 pewter beads then 180 orange beads onto yarn.

With ws facing, and using smaller hook, join with sl st to lower inside edge of left front. Ch 1, tr 183 sts evenly around edge, working 79 up left front, 25 across back neck and 79 down right front. Turn.

Row 2: Ch 1, bdc into each tr of previous row. Break off yarn.

Row 3: Rejoin yarn with sl st to first bdc of Row 2. Ch 1, bdc into each st across. Fasten off.

FINISHING

Lay garment flat with right side facing. Stitch larger button into position on left hand side of cardigan. Place marker on right hand side trim and make 15 ch lp.

Turn the garment inside out and rep above process using smaller button and working 10 ch lp.

Block to required size.

New skills/Making a button loop

Button loops are very quick and easy to make – they can be made separately and stitched into position or worked into the fabric as given below. They are made up of a crochet chain with the ends stitched together side by side.

1 Using yarn and hook as given in pattern, rejoin the yarn to position required.

2 Make chain to required length, ensuring it will fit round the button being used. Remember that the loop will stretch slightly so make it on the small side.

3 Fasten off yarn and stitch end into the wrong side of garment next to where chain started.

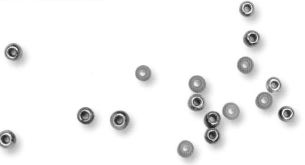

Project 24: Motifs for sweaters

Inspired by plants and flowers, these motifs are a great way to use up all your odd bits of yarn. Have fun with various colour combinations and beads. They are also a good exercise in colour changing, and great for getting to know the various crochet stitches.

before you start

MATERIALS

Yarn A: 25 g (0.8 oz) sport-weight 100% wool (approximately 110 m/ 120 yds per ball) in ginger

Yarn B: 25 g (0.8 oz) laceweight kid-mohair-and-silk blend (approximately 210 m/230 yds per ball) in turquoise

Yarn C: 25 g (0.8 oz) sport-weight lurex (approximately 95 m/ 104 yds per ball) in silver

Yarn D: 25 g (0.8 oz) sport-weight 100% wool (approximately 110 m/ 120 yds per ball) in green

Yarn E: 25 g (0.8 oz) laceweight kid-mohair-and-silk blend (approximately 210 m/230 yds per ball) in lilac

Yarn F: 25 g (0.8 oz) laceweight kid-mohair-and-silk blend (approximately 210 m/230 yds per ball) in cerise

Yarn G: 25 g (0.8 oz) laceweight kid-mohair-and-silk blend (approximately 210 m/230 yds per ball) in lime

Yarn H: 25 g (0.8 oz) sport-weight lurex (approximately 95 m/ 104 yds per ball) in brown

Yarn I: 25 g (0.8 oz) sport-weight 100% wool (approximately 110 m/ 120 yds per ball) in ecru

Yarn J: 25 g (0.8 oz) sport-weight 100% wool (approximately 110 m/ 120 yds per ball) in turquoise

Yarn K: 25 g (0.8 oz) sport-weight lurex (approximately 95 m/ 104 yds per ball) in pink

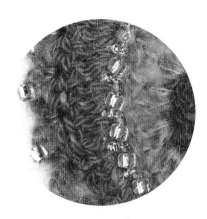

Approximately 100 clear silver-lined 4-mm glass beads

Approximately 20 light blue 4-mm glass beads

HOOK SIZE:

UK 9 (3.5 mm)

ABBREVIATIONS

bch – beaded chain

bdc – beaded double crochet

beg – beginning

btr – beaded treble crochet

ch – chain

dc – double crochet

dtr – double treble crochet

htr – half treble crochet

rep – repeat

rnd – round

rs – right side

sk – skip

sl st – slip stitch

sp(s) – space(s)

st(s) – stitch(es)

tr – treble crochet

ws – wrong side

yo – yarn over

MOTIF 1

TENSION
Round 1 measures 2.5 x 3.2 cm
(1 x 1.25 in.)

FINISHED SIZE
8.2 cm (3.25 in.) square

Thread 10 silver-lined clear beads onto yarn C, set aside.
Thread 16 silver-lined clear beads onto yarn E, set aside.
With yarn A, ch 6, sl st in farthest ch from hook to form a ring.

Rnd 1: Ch 1, 3 dc, 2 htr, 2 tr, 3 dtr, 2 tr, 2 htr, 3 dc, sl st into first dc. Change to yarn B.

Rnd 2: Sl st in first 3 sts, 2 htr, (2 tr into next st) 3 times, 3 dtr into next st, (2 tr into next st) 3 times, 2 htr, 3 sl st, sl st into first sl st of round. Change to pre-beaded yarn C.

Rnd 3: Sl st in first 2 sts, 4 dc, 5 bdc, 3 dc into next st, 5 bdc, 4 dc, 2 sl st, end with sl st into first sl st of round. Change to yarn D.

Rnd 4: Sl st in first 4 sts, 2 dc, (2 dc into next st) 3 times, (2 tr into next st) 4 times, 3 dtr into next st, (2 tr into next st) 4 times, (2 dc into next st) 3 times, 2 dc, 4

sl st, end with sl st into first st of round. Break off yarn.

Rnd 5: With pre-beaded yarn E, join with sl st into first dc of Rnd 4. Ch 1, dc in same st, (ch 2, bch, ch 2, sk next st, dc) 3 times, (ch 1, bch, ch 1, sk next st, dc) 10 times, (ch 2, bch, ch 2, sk next st, dc) 3 times. Fasten off.

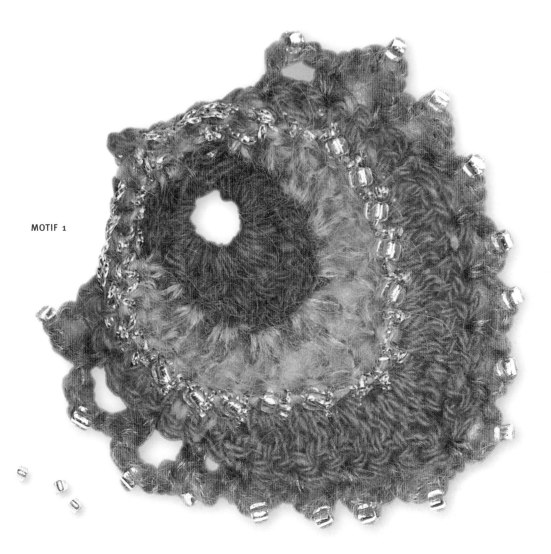

MOTIF 1

MOTIF 2

TENSION
Round 1 measures 5 x 1.25 cm
(2 x 0.5 in.)

FINISHED SIZE
8.2 x 3.75 cm (3.25 x 1.5 in.)

Thread 20 silver-lined clear beads onto yarn D and set aside.

Using yarn F, ch 13.
Row 1: Dc into second ch from hook, 3 htr, 2 tr, 2 htr, 4 dc. Do not turn (12 sts).
Rnd 2 (ws): Change to yarn A. Working in remaining lps of foundation ch, start next rnd at foundation ch and continue around last row. Ch 1, 11 dc, (dc, tr) into next st, (tr, dc) into next stitch, 11 dc, dc into ch at beg of rnd. Change to yarn G.

Rnd 2: Sl st in first dc, 2 dc, 2 htr, 2 tr, 2 htr, 4 dc, 2 tr into next st, 4 dc, 2 htr, 2 tr, 2 htr, 2 dc, 2 sl st. Sl st into first sl st of rnd. Change to pre-beaded yarn D.
Rnd 3: Sl st in first 5 sts, work 6 bdc, (bdc, 2 btr) into next st, (btr, bdc) into next st, 7 bdc, sl st in next 8 sts and in first sl st of rnd. Fasten off yarn.

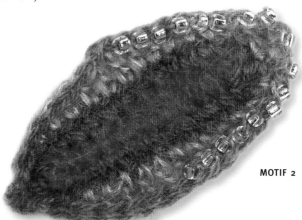

MOTIF 2

MOTIF 3

MOTIF 3

TENSION
Round 1 measures 1 cm (0.375 in.)
across

FINISHED SIZE
8.2 x 5.6 cm (3.25 x 2.25 in.)

Thread 16 silver-lined clear beads onto yarn E and set aside.
Thread 8 silver-lined clear beads onto yarn D and set aside.
Using yarn H, ch 6, sl st in farthest ch from hook to form a ring.
Row 1 (ws): Work 6 dc into ring. Do not join, turn. Change to yarn I.
Row 2 (rs): Ch 2, 2 tr, 2 tr into each of next 2 sts, 2 tr. Turn. Change to yarn F.

Row 3: Ch 2, 3 tr, 2 tr into each of next 2 sts, 3 tr. Turn. Change to beaded yarn E.
Row 4: Ch 2, 2 btr into next st, 2 btr, (2 btr into next st) 4 times, 2 btr, 2 btr into next st. Turn. Change to pre-beaded yarn D.
Row 5: Ch 1, dc, (bdc, dc) 8 times. Sk last st, break off yarn.

Row 6: With rs facing, rejoin yarn C with sl st into beg ring. Work 8 dc along row edges, dc into top corner, *ch 5, sk 1 dc, dc, rep from * 7 times. Work 8 dc along row edges, dc into ring, sl st into first dc of round.

MOTIF 4

TENSION
Round 1 measures 1.8 cm (0.75 in.) across

FINISHED SIZE
5.6 cm (2.25 in.) square

Thread 16 light blue beads onto yarn E and set aside.

Using yarn K, ch 6, sl st in farthest ch from hook to form a ring.
Rnd 1: Ch 1, 16 dc into ring, sl st into first dc.
Rnd 2: Ch 1, dc into same st, dc into next st, *(dc, ch 9, dc) into next st **, dc into next 3 sts; rep from * twice, then from * to ** once more. Dc into next st, sl st to first dc.

Rnd 3: Ch 1, dc into same st, *skip 2 dc, work [2 htr, 17 tr, 2 htr] into next ch 9 lp, sk next 2 dc, dc into next dc, rep from * 3 more times, omitting 1 dc at end of last rep and sl st to first dc of round. Change to pre-beaded yarn E.
Rnd 4: Ch 1, bdc over first st, *ch 5, sk 5 sts, dc into next st, ch 1, bch 1, ch 1, sl st into dc just worked. (Ch 5, sk 4 sts, dc into next st, ch 1, bch 1, ch 1, sl st into dc just worked) twice. Ch 5, sk 5 sts, bdc over next st, rep from * 3 times, omitting bdc at end of last rep and sl st to first bdc of round. Fasten off yarn.

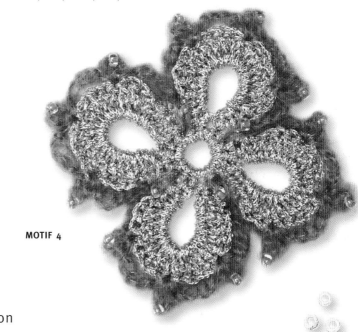

MOTIF 4

New skills/Stitching motifs into position

These motifs are great for jazzing up any type of garment or accessory. The method for stitching the motifs onto your item is the same whether it's a hand-knitted or shop-bought item, though the needle and thread you use may vary.

1 Pin finished motif into required position.

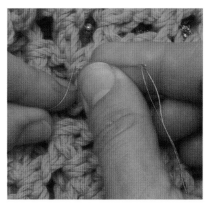

2 Thread sewing needle with thread that tones in with motif, anchor thread at back of garment.

3 Work in backstitch at outer edge of motif until you have worked around the outside of the shape.

Home Accessories

Project 25: Appliqué cushion

Almost too pretty to sit on, this generous cushion is worked in an aran-weight tweedy, natural yarn. The appliqué motifs, worked in a variety of sizes, are simple crochet discs in stripes and solids with contrasting beads to really add texture.

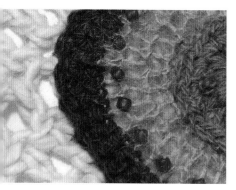

PILLOW PANEL
Make 2.

Using yarn A and larger hook, ch 48.
Row 1: Tr into third ch from hook and in each ch to end (46 tr). Ch 2, turn.
Rows 2–23: Tr into each st across. Ch 2, turn.
Row 24: Tr into each st across. Finish off.
Make a second panel identical to the first.

before you start

MATERIALS

Yarn A: 2 x 100 g (3.5 oz) balls worsted weight 100% wool (approximately 100 m/100 yds per ball) in ecru

Yarn B: 1 x 25 g (0.8 oz) ball worsted weight 100% wool (approximately 100 m/100 yds per ball) in green

Yarn C: 1 x 25 g (0.8 oz) ball laceweight kid-mohair-and-silk blend (approximately 210 m/200 yds per ball) in lilac

Yarn D: 1 x 25 g (0.8 oz) ball worsted weight 100% wool (approximately 100 m/100 yds per ball) in ginger

Yarn E: 1 x 25 g (0.8 oz) ball laceweight kid-mohair-and-silk blend (approximately 210 m/200 yds per ball) in duck-egg blue

Yarn F: 1 x 25 g (0.8 oz) ball worsted weight 100% wool (approximately 100 m/100 yds per ball) in purple

Yarn G: 1 x 25 g (0.8 oz) ball laceweight kid-mohair-and-silk blend

(approximately 210 m/200 yds per ball) in red

Approximately 60 purple beads
Approximately 100 red beads
One 40 cm (16 in.) square pillow form

HOOK SIZES

Main cushion – UK 6 (5.0 mm);
Appliqué motifs – UK 9 (3.5 mm)

TENSION

10 stitches and 6 rows to 10 cm (4 in.) in treble-crochet pattern using larger hook

ABBREVIATIONS

bdc – beaded double crochet
ch – chain
dc – double crochet
rnd – round
sl st – slip stitch
st(s) – stitch(es)
tr – treble crochet

Appliqué cushion motifs

MOTIF 1	MOTIF 2	MOTIF 3	MOTIF 4	MOTIF 5

Thread 15 red beads onto yarn B. With yarn B, ch 6. Sl st in farthest ch from hook to form a ring.

Thread 37 purple beads onto yarn B. With yarn B, ch 6. Sl st in farthest ch from hook to form a ring.

Thread 38 red beads onto yarn D. With yarn D, ch 6. Sl st in farthest ch from hook to form a ring.

Thread 15 purple beads onto yarn F. With yarn F, ch 6. Sl st in farthest ch from hook to form a ring.

(Shown with Motif 6 over centre.) Thread 24 red beads onto yarn E and ch 6. Sl st in farthest ch from hook to form a ring.

 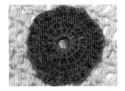 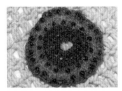  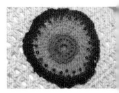

Rnd 1: Ch 1, work 15 dc into ring, join with sl st to first dc of rnd (15 dc).
Rnd 2: Ch 1, (dc, bdc) into each st around, join with sl st to first dc (30 sts).
Fasten off.

Rnd 1: Ch 1, work 15 dc into ring, join with sl st to first dc of rnd (15 dc).
Rnd 2: Ch 1, (dc, bdc) into each st around, join with sl st to first dc (30 sts). Change to yarn C.
Rnd 3: Ch 1, dc into each st around, join with sl st into first dc of rnd.
Rnd 4: Ch 1, dc, *2 dc into the next st, dc in the next st, repeat from * around, ending with sl st into first dc of rnd (45 sts). Change to yarn B.
Rnd 5: Ch 1, dc, *bdc in the next st, dc in the next st, repeat from * around, ending with sl st into first dc of rnd.
Fasten off.

Rnd 1: Ch 1, work 15 dc into ring, join with sl st to first dc of rnd (15 dc).
Rnd 2: Ch 1, (dc, bdc) into each st around, join with sl st to first dc (30 sts). Change to yarn E.
Rnd 3: Ch 1, dc in the first st, *bdc in the next st, dc in the next st, repeat from * around ending sl st into first dc of rnd.
Rnd 4: Ch 1, dc in the first st, *work 2 dc into next st, dc in the next st, repeat from * around, ending with sl st into first dc of rnd (45 sts). Change to yarn B.
Rnd 5: Ch 1, dc in the first st, *bdc in the next st, dc in the next st, repeat from * around, ending with sl st into first dc of rnd.
Fasten off.

Rnd 1: Ch 1, work 15 dc into ring, join with sl st into first dc of rnd (15 sts). Change to yarn G.
Rnd 2: Ch 1, work 2 dc into each st around, ending with sl st into first dc of rnd (30 sts). Change to yarn F.
Rnd 3: Ch 1, dc into each st around, ending with sl st into first st of rnd.
Rnd 4: Ch 1, *dc into next st, bdc in next st, repeat from * around, ending with sl st into first dc of rnd.
Fasten off.

Rnd 1: Ch 1, work 24 dc into ring, join with sl st into first dc of rnd (24 sts).
Rnd 2: Ch 1, work 2 dc into each st around, ending with sl st into first dc of rnd (48 sts).
Rnd 3: Ch 1, dc into each st around, ending with sl st into first st of rnd.
Rnd 4: Ch 1, dc in the first st, *work 2 dc into next st, dc in the next st, repeat from * around, ending with sl st into first dc of rnd (72 sts).
Rnd 5: Repeat rnd 3.
Rnd 6: Ch 1, 2 dc in the next st, *bdc in the next st, dc in the next st, 2 dc in the next st, repeat from * around, ending with sl st into first dc of rnd (96 sts, 24 beads). Change to yarn F.
Rnd 7: Repeat rnd 3.
Rnd 8: Ch 1, 3 dc in the next st, *2 dc in the next st, 3 dc in the next st, repeat from * around, ending with sl st into first dc of rnd (120 sts).
Fasten off.

MOTIF 6

(Shown over centre of Motif 5.) With yarn B, ch 6. Sl st in farthest ch from hook to form a ring.

Rnd 1: Ch 1, work 15 dc into ring, join with sl st into first dc of rnd (15 sts).

Rnd 2: Ch 1, work 2 dc into each st around, ending with sl st into first dc of rnd (30 sts). Fasten off.

MOTIF 7

With yarn F, ch 6. Sl st in farthest ch from hook to form a ring.

Rnd 1: Ch 1, work 15 dc into ring, join with sl st into first dc of rnd (15 sts).

Rnd 2: Ch 1, work 2 dc into each st around, ending with sl st into first dc of rnd (30 sts).

Rnd 3: Ch 1, dc into each st around, ending with sl st into first dc of rnd. Fasten off.

FINISHING

Weave in all ends and tack motifs onto front panel of pillow. With wrong sides facing, sew panels together along 3 sides. Turn right side out, insert pillow form and sew along last side.

Project 26: Beaded throw

Made up of contrasting colours and textured squares to form a chequered look, the soft and light kid-mohair-and-silk yarn works well with the textured tweedy 4-ply pure new wool. The red beads on the squares seem to blend the two colours together. Each square is worked separately so the throw can easily be enlarged.

before you start

MATERIALS

Yarn A: 5 x 25 g (0.8 oz) balls sport-weight wool (approximately 110 m/120 yds per ball) in grey
Yarn B: 3 x 25 g (0.8 oz) balls laceweight kid-mohair-and-silk blend (approximately 210 m/ 230 yds per ball) in red
Approximately 700 red beads

HOOK SIZE

UK 9 (3.5mm)

TENSION

10 cm (4 in.) per square motif

FINISHED SIZE

72 cm (28 in.) by 90 cm (36 in.)

ABBREVIATIONS

btr – beaded treble crochet
btr2tog – beaded treble crochet 2 together
btr3tog – beaded treble crochet 3 together
ch – chain
dc – double crochet
lp(s) – loop(s)
rep – repeat
rnd – round
sl st – slip stitch
tr – treble crochet
ws – wrong side
yo – yarn over

MOTIF

Thread beads onto yarn A. Make 32 beaded squares in yarn A and 31 unbeaded squares in yarn B.
Ch 6, join to form ring.

Rnd 1: Ch 1, (dc into ring, ch 15) 12 times, sl st to first dc.

Rnd 2: Sl st along in first 4 ch of ch 15 lp, ch 3, btr2tog into same lp as follows: bring bead up to hook, (yo, insert hook in lp, yo, pull up a lp, yo pull through two lps) twice, yo, pull through all lps on hook. Btr2tog made. *Ch 4, btr3tog into same lp as follows: bring bead up to hook, (yo, insert hook in lp, yo, pull up a lp, yo pull through two lps) three times, yo, pull through all lps on hook. Btr3tog made. (Ch 4, dc into next lp) twice, ch 4, btr3tog into next lp, rep from * 3 more times, omitting btr3tog at end of last rep, sl st into first btr group.

Rnd 3: Sl st into corner lp, ch 3, btr2tog into same lp, * ch 4, btr3tog into same lp, (ch 4, dc into next ch lp, ch 4, btr3tog into next lp) twice, rep from * 3 times more, omitting btr3tog at end of last rep, sl st into first btr group of rnd.
Fasten off.

JOINING

Using one motif of each colour, hold motifs with ws together and yarn A motif facing you. Join yarn A with sl st in upper right corner lp of yarn A motif. Dc in same lp, ch 1. Dc in corresponding corner lp of yarn B motif behind. *Ch 1, dc in next ch lp of yarn A motif, ch 1, dc in next ch lp of yarn B motif. Rep from * until upper left corner of yarn B motif has been worked.
Fasten off.

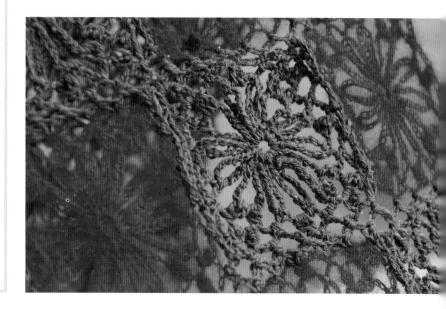

Project 27: Circular motif cushion

This project is chunky, funky and fun! Worked using a super-size pure new wool, you will have made the front and back in no time. The fun feel to this cushion is also echoed with the addition of brightly coloured wooden beads.

before you start

MATERIALS

3 x 100 g (3.5 oz) balls bulky weight 100% wool (approximately 80 m/87 yds per ball) in ecru
Approximately 200 4-mm red wooden beads
Approximately 50 10-mm multi-coloured wooden beads
One 50 cm (20 in.) diameter round pillow form

HOOK SIZE

UK 0 (9.0 mm)

TENSION

7 sts and 3 rows to 10 cm (4 in.)

FINISHED SIZE

50 cm (20 in.) diameter

ABBREVIATIONS

beg – beginning
ch – chain
dc – double crochet
rnd – round
sl st – slip stitch
st(s) – stitch(es)
tr – treble crochet

PILLOW PANEL
Make 2.

Ch 6, sl st in farthest ch from hook to form a ring.

Rnd 1: Ch 2, work 12 tr into ring, sl st into ch 2 at beg of rnd (12 tr).

Rnd 2: Ch 2, work 2 tr into each tr of previous rnd, sl st into ch 2 at beg of rnd (24 tr).

Rnd 3: Ch 2, *2 tr into next st, tr into the next st, repeat from * around, sl st into beg ch 2 (36 tr),

Rnd 4: Ch 2, *2 tr into next st, tr into next 2 sts, repeat from * sl st into beg ch 2 (48 tr).

Rnd 5: Ch 2, *2 tr into next st, tr into next 3 sts, repeat from * sl st into beg ch 2 (60 tr).

Rnd 6: Ch 2, *2 tr into next st, tr into next 4 sts, repeat from * sl st into beg ch 2 (72 tr).

Rnd 7: Ch 2, *2 tr into next st, tr into next 5 sts, repeat from * sl st into beg ch 2 (84 tr). Finish off.

FRONT PANEL BEADING

Stitch 1 red bead to top of each tr on rnd 2.
Stitch 1 multicoloured bead to top of every third tr on rnd 3.
Stitch 1 red bead to top of each tr on rnd 4.
Stitch 1 multicoloured bead to top of every fourth tr on rnd 5
Stitch 1 red bead to top of every tr on rnd 6.

ASSEMBLY

Place front and back panels so that wrong sides are facing. In any st of rnd 7, insert hook in a st from both the front and back panel at the same time, and join with a sl st. Ch 1, dc in the same st and in each st around, making sure to catch both the front and back panels in each st.

Once you have worked approximately halfway around the edge, insert the pillow form and complete the rnd as before, ending with a sl st in the first dc of rnd. Finish off and weave in ends.

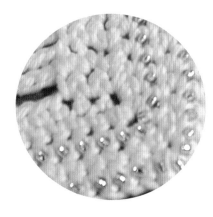

Project 28: Beaded mat

These place settings are fun and easy to make. Crocheted in worsted-weight cotton yarn, they can be easily popped in the washing machine. Change the colours to coordinate them with your favourite crockery or dining area décor.

before you start

MATERIALS

50 g (1.75 oz) worsted-weight cotton (approximately 58 m/64 yds per ball) in cream
Approximately 350 silver-lined glass beads

HOOK SIZE

UK 6 (5.0 mm)

TENSION

8.5 cm (3.25 in.) across one stitch repeat, 11 rows per 7.5 cm (3 in.)

FINISHED SIZE

30 x 20 cm (12 x 8 in.)

ABBREVIATIONS

bdc – beaded double crochet
ch – chain
dc – double crochet
lp – loop
rep – repeat
rnd – round
sk – skip
sl st – slip stitch
st(s) – stitch(es)
tr – treble crochet

PATTERN

Row 1: Ch 46, dc in second ch from hook and in each ch to end, turn (45 dc).
Row 2: Ch 1, dc in first 3 sts, *ch 5, (sk 2, tr in next st) 3 times, ch 5, sk 2, dc in next 3 sts. Rep from * across, turn.
Row 3: Ch 1, dc in first 3 sts, *ch 5, dc in ch lp, dc in next 3 tr, dc in ch loop, ch 5, dc in next 3 dc. Rep from * across, turn.
Row 4: Ch 1, dc in first 3 sts, *ch 5, sk first dc, dc in next 3 dc, sk next dc, ch 5, dc in next 3 dc. Rep from * across, turn.
Row 5: Ch 1, dc in first 3 sts, *(ch 2, tr in next dc) 3 times ch 2, dc in next 3 dc. Rep from * across, turn.
Row 6: Ch 1, dc across, working a dc in each dc, 2 dc in each ch lp, and dc in each tr. Turn (45 dc).
Rows 7–21: Rep rows 2 through 6 three more times, then break off yarn.

BORDER

String all beads onto yarn.
Rnd 1: With wrong side facing, join with sl st in any st. Ch 1, dc in each st and end of each row around, working 3 dc in the corners. Do not turn.
Rnd 2: Ch 1, bdc in each st around, working 3 bdc in each corner.
Rnd 3: Ch 1, dc in each st around, working 3 dc in each corner.
Rnd 4: Rep rnd 2.

Finish off and weave in ends.

Project 29: Floor cushion

This textured floor cushion is worked in a beautiful pure new wool, aran-weight tweedy yarn. The chequer-board pattern is created by working evenly around the front or back of the stitches. The centre panels have been framed with a simple beaded border worked in separate sections.

before you start

MATERIALS
6 x 50 g (1.75 oz) balls worsted-weight 100% wool (approximately 113 m/123 yds per ball) in green
800 clear glass beads
60 cm (24 in.) square pillow form

HOOK SIZE
UK 6 (5.0 mm)

TENSION
13 stitches and 8 rows to 10 cm (4 in.) over textured pattern

FINISHED SIZE
58 cm (23 in.) square

ABBREVIATIONS
bdc – beaded double crochet
bptr – back post treble crochet
ch – chain
dc – double crochet
fptr – front post treble crochet
rep – repeat
rnd – round
rs – right side
sl st – slip stitch
st(s) – stitch(es)
tr – treble crochet
ws – wrong side
yo – yarn over

TEXTURED PATTERN (FRONT PANEL)
Ch 64.

Row 1 (ws): Tr into third ch from the hook and in each ch to end. Turn.

Row 2 (rs): Ch 2, miss first st * 4 fptr, 4 bptr, rep from * 6 more times. 4 fptr, tr into top of turning ch.

Row 3: Ch 2, miss first st * 4 bptr, 4 fptr, rep from * 6 times. 4 bptr, ending with tr into top of turning ch.

Row 4: Rep row 2.

Row 5: Rep row 2.

Row 6: Rep row 3.

Row 7: Rep row 2.

Rows 8–37: Rep rows 2–7 another 5 times.

BEADED BORDER
Thread beads onto yarn.

With ws of work facing, join with sl st to lower right hand corner and work up the right hand side.

Rnd 1 (rs): Ch 1, work 2 bdc around post of tr at end of row 1, * bdc around post of next tr at end of next row, 2 bdc around post of tr at end of next row, rep from * up side of piece. Work 3 bdc in corner, bdc in each tr across top, 3 bdc in corner, 2 bdc around post of tr in row 37, rep from * to * down third side. Work 3 bdc in corner, bdc in unworked lps of beginning ch, 3 bdc in last corner. Join with sl st to first bdc of rnd.

Rnd 2 (ws): Ch 1, dc into each bdc of previous round, working 3 dc into each corner, join with sl st to first dc of rnd.

Rnd 3: Ch 1, bdc into each dc of previous round, working 3 bdc into each corner, join with sl st into first bdc of rnd.
Rnd 4: Rep rnd 2.
Rnd 5: Rep rnd 3.
Fasten off and weave in ends.

BACK PANEL
Ch 61.
Row 1: Tr into third ch from hook and in each ch to end (60 sts includes turning ch).
Row 2: Ch 2, turn. Tr into each st across.
Rows 3–28: Rep row 2.

DOUBLE CROCHET BORDER
With ws of work facing, join with sl st to lower right hand corner and work up the right hand side.
Rnd 1: Ch 1, work 2 dc around post of tr at end of row 1, *dc around post of tr at end of next row, 2 dc around post of tr at end of next row, rep from * up side of piece. Work 3 dc in corner, dc in each tr across top, 3 dc in corner, 2 dc around post of tr at end of row 37, rep from * to * down third side. Work 3 dc in corner, dc in unworked lps of beginning ch, 3 dc in last corner. Join with sl st to first dc of rnd.
Rnd 2: Ch 1, dc into each dc of previous rnd, working 3 dc into each corner, join with sl st to first dc of rnd.
Rnds 3–5: Rep rnd 2.
Fasten off yarn and weave in ends.

FINISHING
With ws of panels held together, sew along 3 sides. Insert pillow form and sew up last side.

New skills/Front and back stem treble crochet stitch

This is a technique used to add texture and pattern to your crochet fabric by simply working crochet stitches around either the front or back of the stem of the stitch in the row below.

Front post treble crochet

1 Yarn over as normal, insert hook from the front right to left around the back of the stem of the stitch instead of into the top, yarn over and draw round stem, back to start position.

2 Yarn over and complete double as normal.

Back post treble

1 Yarn over as normal, insert hook from the back right to left around the front of the stem of the stitch instead of into the top, yarn over and draw round stem, back to start position.

2 Yarn over and complete treble as normal.

Project 30: Coasters

This project is quick and easy to make and the beaded DK cotton gives a nice weight to the coasters. It's also a fun way to use up all your odd bits of wool, using different types of yarn to truly make them your own.

before you start

MATERIALS

For 2 coasters, one 50 g (1.75 oz) ball DK-weight 100% cotton (approximately 89 m/97 yds per ball) in ecru

Approximately 70 beads for edge-only coaster

Approximately 150 beads for panel coaster

HOOK SIZE

UK 8 (4.0 mm)

TENSION

Round 1 measures 5 cm (2 in.) across between ch 2 loops

FINISHED SIZE

Approximately 12.5 cm (5 in.) square

ABBREVIATIONS

bdc – beaded double crochet
beg cl – beginning cluster
ch – chain
cl – cluster
dc – double crochet
sl st – slip stitch
sp – space
tr – treble crochet
yo – yarn over

BEADED EDGE COASTER

Thread 70 beads onto yarn. Ch 8, join with sl st in farthest ch from hook to make a ring.

Rnd 1: Make beg cl into ring as follows: ch 3, *yo, insert hook, yo, pull up a loop, yo pull through 2 loops on hook, repeat from * once, yo, pull through all 3 loops on hook. Beg cl made. Ch 5.
Make cl as follows: repeat from * to * 3 times, yo, pull through all 4 loops on hook. Cl made. Ch 2, (cl, ch 5, cl, ch 2) three more times. Join with sl st in 3rd ch of beg cl.
Rnd 2: Sl st into first ch 5 sp, (beg cl, ch 2, cl) in same sp, ch 2, 3 dc into the next ch 2 sp, ch 2, *(cl, ch 2, cl) into ch 5 sp, ch 2, 3 dc into next ch 2 sp, ch 2, rep from * around. Join with sl st to 3rd ch of beg cl.
Rnd 3: Sl st into first ch 2 sp, (beg cl, ch 2, cl) in same sp, *ch 2, 2 dc into ch 2 sp, dc into each of the next 3 dc, 2 dc into next ch 2 sp, ch 2, (cl, ch 2, cl) in ch 2 sp, rep from * around. Join with sl st into 3rd ch of beg cl.
Rnd 4: Sl st into first ch 2 sp, (beg cl, ch 2, cl) in same sp, *ch 2, 2 dc into ch 2 sp, dc into each of the next 7 dc, 2 dc into next ch 2 sp, ch 2, (cl, ch 2, cl) in ch 2 sp, rep from * around. Join with sl st into 3rd ch of beg cl.
Rnd 5: Sl st into first ch 2 sp, (beg cl, ch 2, cl) in same sp, *ch 2, 2 bdc into ch 2 sp, bdc into each of the next 11 dc, 2 bdc into next ch 2 sp, ch 2, (cl, ch 2, cl) in ch 2 sp, rep from * around. Join with sl st into 3rd ch of beg cl. Fasten off yarn.

BEADED PANEL COASTER

Thread 150 beads onto yarn. Ch 8, join with sl st in farthest ch from hook to make a ring.

Rnd 1: Make beg cl into ring: ch 3, *yo, insert hook, yo, pull up a loop, yo pull through 2 loops on hook, repeat from * once, yo, pull through all 3 loops on hook. Beg cl made. Ch 5.
Make cl: repeat from * to * 3 times, yo, pull through all 4 loops on hook. Cl made. Ch 2, (cl, ch 5, cl, ch 2) three more times. Join with sl st in 3rd ch of beg cl.
Rnd 2: Sl st into first ch 5 sp, (beg cl, ch 2, cl) in same sp, ch 2, 3 bdc into the next ch 2 sp, ch 2, *(cl, ch 2, cl) into ch 5 sp, ch 2, 3 dc into next ch 2 sp, ch 2, rep from * around. Join with sl st to 3rd ch of beg cl.
Rnd 3: Sl st into first ch 2 sp, (beg cl, ch 2, cl) in same sp, *ch 2, 2 bdc into ch 2 sp, bdc into each of the next 3 dc, 2 bdc into next ch 2 sp, ch 2, (cl, ch 2, cl) in ch 2 sp, rep from * around. Join with sl st into 3rd ch of beg cl.
Rnd 4: Sl st into first ch 2 sp, (beg cl, ch 2, cl) in same sp, *ch 2, 2 bdc into ch 2 sp, bdc into each of the next 7 dc, 2 bdc into next ch 2 sp, ch 2, (cl, ch 2, cl) in ch2 sp, rep from * around. Join with sl st into 3rd ch of beg cl.
Rnd 5: Sl st into first ch 2 sp, (beg cl, ch 2, cl) in same sp, *ch 2, 2 bdc into ch 2 sp, bdc into each of the next 11 dc, 2 bdc into next ch 2 sp, ch 2, (cl, ch 2, cl) in ch 2 sp, rep from * around. Join with sl st into 3rd ch of beg cl. Fasten off yarn.

Trims

If you want to liven up a plain or shop-bought item — whether a garment, wearable accessory or home accessory, try making or adapting these trims. In no time at all, you'll have the length you need, and then you can simply attach it by sewing or crocheting it on for instant results that look great! Change the yarn and bead colours to complement your item.

Beaded trim 1

MATERIALS

Yarn A: sport-weight 100% wool (approximately 110 m/120 yds per ball) in dark purple

Yarn B: 25 g (0.8 oz) laceweight kid-mohair-and-silk blend (approximately 210 m/230 yds per ball) in violet

Two 10-mm glass beads per 2.5 cm (1 in.) of trim length

FINISHED SIZE

2 repeats per 2.5 cm (1 in.), 2.5 cm (1 in.) wide

ABBREVIATIONS

bch – beaded chain
ch – chain
dc – double crochet
lp – loop
sk – skip

PATTERN

Row 1: Using yarn A, ch a multiple of 3 sts. Dc in 6th ch from hook. (Ch 2, sk 2, dc in next ch) across. Fasten off.

Row 2: Using double strand of yarn B as one, thread beads onto yarn. * Work (2 dc, ch, bch, ch, 2 dc in same lp) across. Fasten off.

PATTERN

Using yarn A, ch a multiple of 3 sts plus 1.

Row 1: Dc in 2nd ch from hook and each ch to end, turn.

Row 2: Ch 1, dc in back lp of each st across, turn.

Row 3: Ch 1, dc in front lp of each st across. Fasten off.

Thread beads onto yarn B.

Row 4: Using yarn B, dc in first 2 sts, bdc in next st, (ch 10, sk 5 sts, bch in next st across. Fasten off.

Row 5: Using yarn C, dc in 1st dc of row 4.
(Ch 10, sk 5 sts of row 3, dc in next st) across.

Beaded trim 2

MATERIALS

Yarn A: sport-weight 100% wool (approximately 110 m/120 yds per ball) in lavender

Yarn B: sport-weight 100% wool (approximately 110 m/120 yds per ball) in pink

Yarn C: sport-weight 100% wool (approximately 110 m/120 yds per ball) in red

10-mm beads, 1 per 2.5 cm (1 in.) of trim length

FINISHED SIZE

1 repeat per 2.5 cm (1 in.) 3.75 cm (1.5 in.) wide

ABBREVIATIONS

bdc – beaded double crochet
ch – chain
dc – double crochet
lp – loop
sk – skip
st(s) – stitch(es)

Beaded trim 3

MATERIALS

25 g (0.8 oz) ball sport-weight 100% wool (approximately 110 m/ 120 yds per ball) in pink
Small white beads, 10 per 2.5 cm (1 in.) of trim length

FINISHED SIZE

3 repeats per 20 cm (8 in.), 4.5 cm (1.75 in.) wide

ABBREVIATIONS

bdc – beaded double crochet
ch – chain
dc – double crochet
dec – decrease
lp – loop
rs – right side
ws – wrong side

PATTERN

Row 1 (rs): Ch 5, dc in 2nd ch from hook and each across, turn (4 dc).

Row 2 (ws): Ch 1, decrease (dec) as follows: (insert hook in next st and pull up a loop) twice, yo, pull through all 3 lps on hook. Dec made. Dc in next st, 2 dc in last st, turn (4 sts).

Row 3: Ch 1, 2 dc in first st, dc in next, dec across next 2 sts, turn (4 sts).

Row 4: Repeat row 2.
Row 5: Repeat row 3.
Row 6: Repeat row 2
Row 7: Ch 1, dc in each st across, turn (4 sts).
Row 8: Repeat row 3.
Row 9: Repeat row 2.
Row 10: Repeat row 3.
Row 11: Repeat row 2.
Row 12: Repeat row 3.
Row 13: Repeat row 7.
Repeat rows 2–13 until trim is desired length.

CIRCLES

Make one per 2.5 cm (1 in.) of finished trim length. Using either yarn A or B, ch 4, join with sl st in ch farthest from hook to form ring.

Rnd 1: Ch 1, work 8 dc in ring, join with sl st to first dc of round.
Rnd 2: Ch 1, 2 dc in each st around, join with sl st to first dc of round. Finish off.

TRIM

Thread beads onto yarn C.

Row 1: Using yarn C, (ch 7, dc in any edge st of a circle) to desired length, ending ch 8, turn.
Rows 2–4: Sk first ch, (7 dc, bdc) across, ending with 7 dc, turn. Fasten off at end of row 4.

Beaded trim 4

MATERIALS

Yarn A: sport-weight 100% wool (approximately 110 m/120 yds per ball) in rose
Yarn B: sport-weight 100% wool (approximately 110 m/120 yds per ball) in red
Yarn C: sport-weight 100% wool (approximately 110 m/120 yds per ball) in pink
Small red beads, 3 per 2.5 cm (1 in.) of trim length

FINISHED SIZE

1 repeat per 2.5 cm (1 in.), 4.5 cm (1.5 in.) wide

ABBREVIATIONS

bch—beaded chain
ch—chain
dc—double crochet
sk—skip

Yarn directory

Below is a list of the specific yarns and beads used to make the projects. However, if you cannot find any of these yarns or simply wish to make a project in a different yarn, use the information supplied at the beginning of each project, where you will find the quantity, weight and fibre content of the yarns. Additional advice on substituting yarns can be found on pages 12–13.

WEARABLE ACCESSORIES

Project 1: Beaded ruffle scarf
Yarns: Rowan kid classic: 847 (cherry red); Rowan kidsilk haze 595 (liqueur).
Beads: 100 multicoloured large glass beads.

Project 2: Lace-effect shawl
Yarns: Rowan DK felted tweed 146 (herb); Rowan kidsilk haze 585 (nightly); Rowan kidsilk haze 582 (trance); Rowan kidsilk haze 597 (jelly); Rowan kidsilk haze 592 (heavenly).
Beads: Rowan j3001008.

Project 3: Wrist warmers
Yarn: Rowan kidsilk haze 582 (trance).
Beads: Rowan j3001006.

Project 4: Pashmina
Yarns: Rowan kid classic 840 (crystal); Rowan kidsilk haze 589 (majestic); Rowan kidsilk haze 592 (heavenly).
Beads: Rowan j3001014.

Project 5: Beaded string bag
Yarn: Rowan handknit DK cotton 318 (seafarer).
Beads: Nottingham bead company: purple 8 mm wooden beads; pink 6 mm wooden beads; natural 10 mm wooden beads.

Project 6: Shoulder bag
Yarns: Rowan big wool 007 (smoky); Rowan big wool 008 (black); Rowan kidsilk haze 600 (dewberry).
Beads: Approx. 120 pewter glass beads.

Project 7: Evening bag
Yarn: Rowan cotton glace 816 (mocha choc).
Beads: Beadworks: 240 dark turquoise glass beads; 280 green glass beads; 220 silvery green glass beads.

Project 8: Flower pin corsage
Yarns: Rowan Yorkshire tweed 4-ply 286 (graze); Rowan Yorkshire tweed 4-ply 268 (enchant); Rowan kidsilk haze 605 (smoke).
Beads: Rowan j3001017.

Project 9: Beaded beanie
Yarn: Rowan DK wool cotton 900 (antique).
Beads: Rowan j3001022.

Project 10: Twenties-inspired scarf
Yarn: Rowan kidsilk haze 581 (meadow)
Beads: Approx. 280 matte green glass beads (Rowan j3001022).

Project 11: Beaded beret
Yarn: Rowan 4-ply soft 370 (whisper).
Beads: Approx 260 pewter glass beads (Rowan j3001006).

Project 12: Textured beaded bag
Yarns: Rowan summer tweed 526 (angel); Rowan summer tweed 528 (brilliant).
Beads: Nottingham beads company: 144 pink 8mm wooden beads.

Project 13: Beaded necklace
Yarn: Rowan lurex shimmer 333 (pewter).
Beads: Rowan j3001006.

Project 14: Earflap hat
Yarns: Rowan Yorkshire tweed chunky 557 (olive oil); Rowan kidsilk haze 582 (trance); Rowan kidsilk haze 584 (villain); Rowan kidsilk haze 592 (heavenly); Rowan kidsilk haze 581 (meadow); Rowan kidsilk haze 588 (drab).
Beads: 50 multicoloured, mixed-size glass beads.

Project 15: Beaded head band
Yarn: Rowan handknit DK cotton 251 (ecru).
Beads: Rowan j3001017.

Project 16: Brooch and pendant
Yarn: Rowan Yorkshire tweed 4-ply 264 (barley).
Beads: 9 medium glass beads – various colours; Beadworks: 9 orange small beads.

GARMENTS

Project 17: Box crew-neck
Yarn: Rowan wool cotton 952 (hiss); Rowan 4-ply soft 387 (rain cloud).
Beads: Rowan j3001006.

Project 18: Slash-neck vest
Yarn: Rowan summer tweed 537 (summer berry).
Beads: Nottingham bead company: 60 purple 6 mm beads.

Project 19: Halter-neck top
Yarn: Rowan cotton glace 811 (tickle).
Beads: Approx. 70 purple (Rowan j3001014); approx. 70 blue (Rowan j3001013).

Project 20: Cobweb shrug
Yarn: Rowan kidsilk haze 582 (trance).
Beads: Rowan j3001006.

Project 21: Beaded tunic
Yarns: Rowan cotton rope 062 (fruit gum); Rowan handknit DK cotton 303 (sugar)
Beads: Approx. 400 white beads (Rowan j3001016).

Project 22: Bikini top
Yarn: Rowan denim 225 (Nashville)
Beads: Approx. 250 turquoise glass beads (Rowan j3001013).

Project 23: Cap-sleeved wrap
Yarn: Rowan cotton glace 730 (Oyster)
Beads: 248 pewter beads (Rowan j3001006); Beadworks: 248 orange beads.

Project 24: Motifs for sweaters
Yarns: Rowan Yorkshire tweed 4-ply 273 (glory); Rowan Yorkshire tweed 4-ply 286 (graze); C: Rowan Yorkshire tweed 4-ply 271 (cheerful); Rowan Yorkshire tweed 4-ply 263 (dessicated); Rowan kidsilk haze 600 (dewberry); Rowan kidsilk haze 582 (trance); Rowan kidsilk haze 606 (candy girl); Rowan kidsilk haze 597 (jelly); Rowan lurex shimmer 336 (gleam); Rowan lurex shimmer 333 (pewter); Rowan lurex shimmer 335 (bronze).

HOME ACCESSORIES

Project 25: Appliqué cushion
Yarn: Rowan Yorkshire tweed aran 417 (tusk); Rowan Yorkshire tweed 4-ply 273 (glory); Rowan Yorkshire tweed 4-ply 286 (graze); Rowan kidsilk haze 606 (candy girl); Rowan kidsilk haze 582 (trance); Rowan kidsilk haze 600 (dewberry).
Beads: Approx. 80 purple (Rowan j3001019); Approx. 60 red (Rowan j3001018).

Project 26: Beaded throw
Yarns: Rowan Yorkshire tweed 4-ply 268 (enchant); Rowan kidsilk haze 606 (candy girl).
Beads: Rowan j3001018.

Project 27: Circular cushion
Yarn: Rowan big wool 001 (hot white).
Beads: Nottingham beads company: 152 red wooden 4 mm beads.

Project 28: Beaded mat
Yarn: Rowan handknit DK cotton 251 (ecru).
Beads: Beadworks: clear, small glass beads.

Project 29: Floor cushion
Yarn: Rowan Yorkshire tweed DK 347 (skip).
Beads: Rowan j3001008.

Project 30: Coasters
Yarn: Rowan handknit DK cotton 205 (ecru)
Beads: Rowan j3001022; Rowan j3001019; Beadworks: small orange glass beads.

Trims
Yarns: Rowan cotton glace 816 (mocha choc); Rowan kidsilk haze 600 (dewberry); Rowan cotton glace 811 (tickle); Rowan handknit cotton 215 (rosso); Rowan handknit cotton 303 (slick); Rowan lurex shimmer 336 (gleam); Rowan kidsilk haze 606 (hot pink); Rowan kidsilk haze 596 (marmalade); Rowan kidsilk haze 583 (blushes); Rowan kidsilk haze (shell); Rowan cotton glace 747 (candy girl).
Beads: John Lewis Partnership: mix of multi-shaped glass beads; Rowan 3001018; Rowan j300101016.

Resources

ENGLAND

NORTH EAST

Burn & Walton
Parkside Place
Bellingham
Hexham NE48 2AY
01434 220 395
burnwalton@aol.com

Ring a Rosie
69 Front Street
Monkseaton
Tyne and Wear NE25 8AA
0191 252 8874

Village Craft Shop
37 North Road
Boldon Colliery
Tyne and Wear NE35 8AZ
0191 519 1645

The Wool Shop
13 Castlegate
Berwick upon Tweed TD15 1JS
01289 306 104

NORTH WEST

And Sew What
247 Eaves Lane
Chorley
Lancashire PR6 0AG
01257 267 438
www.sewwhat.gb.com

Fun 2 Do
21 Scotch Street
Carlisle
Cumbria CA3 8PY
01228 523 843
www.fun2do.co.uk

Marchmoon Limited
73 Avondale Road
Liverpool L15 3HF
01704 577 415

Spinning a Yarn
46 Market Street
Ulverston
Cumbria LA12 7LS
01229 581 020
www.spinningayarn.com

Stash
4 Godstall Lane
Chester
Cheshire CH1 1LN
01244 311 136
www.celticove.com

Victoria Grant
Waterways
High Street
Uppermill, Oldham
Lancashire OL3 6HT
01457 870 756

YORKSHIRE

Attica 2
Commercial Street
Hebden Bridge
West Yorkshire HX7 8AJ

Bobbins
Wesley Hall
Church Street
Whitby
North Yorkshire YO22 4DE
01947 600 585

Busy Hands
Unit 16 Ashbrook Park
Parkside Lane
Leeds LS11 5SF
0113 272 0851

Jenny Scott's Creative Embroidery
The Old Post Office
39 Duke Street
Settle BD24 9DJ
01729 824 298

Noctule
50 Gillygate
York
North Yorkshire YO31 7EQ
01904 610 043

EAST MIDLANDS

Bee Inspired Limited
The Old Post Office
236 Windmill Avenue
Kettering
Northamptonshire NN1 7DQ
01536 514 646

Heirs and Graces
The Square
Bakewell
Derbyshire DE45 1DA
01629 815 873

The Knitting Workshop
23 Trowell Grove
Long Eaton
Nottingham NG10 4A
0115 946 8370

Quorn Country Crafts
18 Churchgate
Loughborough
Leicestershire LE11 1UD
01509 211 604

Taylor's Teddies
4a Graham Road
Great Malvern
Worcestershire WR14 2HN
01684 572 760

EAST ANGLIA

Arts & Crafts
Tunstead Road
Hoveton
Wroxham
Norfolk NR12 8QG
01603 783 505

D & P Colchester
The Barn
South Lodge Farm
Low Road
Great Plumstead
Norwich NR13 5ED
01603 721 466

Sew Creative
97 King Street
Cambridge CB1 1LD
01223 350 691

WEST MIDLANDS

Cucumberpatch Limited
13 March Avenue
Wolstanton
Staffordshire ST5 8BB
01782 878 234
www.cucumberpatch.co.uk

K2Tog
97 High Street
Wolstanton
Newcastle under Lyme
Staffordshire ST5 0EP
01782 862 332

Natural Knits
Hoar Park Craft Village
B4114 Ansley
Warwickshire CV10 0QU
0121 748 7981

Web of Wool
53 Regent Grove
Holly Walk
Leamington Spa
Warwick CV32 4PA
01926 311 614

SOUTH EAST

Battle Wool Shop
2 Mount Street
Battle
East Sussex TN33 0EG
01424 775 073

Burford Needlecraft
117 High Street
Burford
Oxfordshire OX18 4RG
01993 822 136

Creations
79 Church Road
Barnes
London SW13 9HH

Creations
29 Turnham Green Terrace
Chiswick
London W4 1RG

Gades
Victoria Plaza
242 Churchill South
Southend on Sea
Essex SS2 5SD
01702 613 789

Irene Noad
1 Farnham Road
Bishops Stortford
Hertfordshire CM23 1JJ
01279 653 701

Kangaroo
70 High Street
Lewes
East Sussex BN7 1XG
01273 478 554

The Knit Tin
2 Fountain Court
Olney
Buckinghamshire MK46 4BB
01234 714 300

Loop
41 Cross Street
Islington
London N1 2BB
020 7288 1160
www.loop.gb.com

Myfanwy Hart
Winifred Cottage
17 Elms Road
Fleet
Hampshire GU15 3EG
01252 617 667

Pandora
196 High Street
Guildford
Surrey GU1 3HZ
01483 572 558
www.stitch1knit1.com

Portmeadow Designs
104 Walton Street
Oxford
Oxfordshire OX2 6EB
01865 311 008

**Shoreham Knitting &
Needlecraft**
19 East Street
Shoreham-by-Sea
West Sussex BN43 5ZE
01273 461 029
www.englishyarns.co.uk

Taj Yarn & Crafts
2 Wellesey Avenue
Richings Park
Iver
Buckinghamshire S10 9AY
01753 653 900

Thread Bear
350 Limpsfield Road
South Croydon CR2 9BX
0208 657 5050

Yummies
91 Queens Park Road
Brighton
East Sussex BN2 0GJ
01273 672 632
South West

Cottage Yarns
Glebe Land
Aveton
Gifford
Kingsbridge
Devon TQ7 4LX
01548 550 741

Divine Design
Libra Court
Fore Street
Sidmouth
Devon EX10 8AJ
07967 127 273

Knitting Corner
9 Pepper Street
149–150 East Reach
Taunton
Somerset TA1 3HT
01823 284 768

Sally Carr Designs
The Yarn Shop
31 High Street
Totnes
Devon TQ9 5NP
01803 863 060

The Wool & Craft Shop Ltd
Swanage
Dorset BH19 1AB
01929 422 814

WALES

B's Hive
20–22 Church Street
Monmouth
Gwent NP25 3BU
01600 713 548

Clare's
13 Great Darkgate Street
Aberystwyth SY23 1DE
01970 617 786

Colourway
Market Street
Whitland SA34 0AH
01994 241 333
www.colourway.co.uk
shop@colourway.co.uk

Copperfield
Four Mile Bridge Road
Valley
Anglesey LL65 3HV
01407 740 982

Mrs Mac's
2 Woodville Road
Mumbles
Swansea SA3 4AD
01792 369 820

SCOTLAND

CE Cross Stitch
Narvik
Weyland Terrace
Kirkwall
Orkney KW15 1LS
01856 879 049

Cormack's and Crawford's
56–57 High Street
Dingwall
Ross-shire IV15 9HL
01349 562 234

Di Gilpin
Hansa Close
Burghers Close
141 South Street
St Andrews
Fife KY16 9UN
01334 476 193
www.handknitwear.com

Elizabeth Lovick
Harbour View
Front Road
Orkney KW17 2SL
01603 783 505

Fibres
133 Commercial Street
Lerwick
Shetland ZE1 0DL
01595 695 575

Galloway Knitwear
6 Manx View
Port William
Dumfries & Galloway DG8 9SA
01988 700 789

HK Handknit
83 Bruntsfield Place
Edinburgh EH10 4HG
0131 228 1551
www.handknit.co.uk

Hume Sweet Hume
Pierowall Village
Westray
Orkney KW17 2DH
01857 677 259

The Knitting Parlour
The Park
Findliorn Bay
Forres
Moray IV36 0TZ
01684 527 760

Patterns of Light
Kishorn
Strathcarron
Wester-ross IV54 8XB
01520 733 363

Phoenix Centre
The Park, Findliorn Bay
Forres
Moray IV36 0TZ
01309 690 110

Pie in the Skye
Ferry View, Armadale Bay
Sleat
Isle of Skye IV45 8RS
01471 844 370

Ragamuffin
278 Canon Gate
The Royal Mile
Edinburgh EH8 8AA
0131 557 6007

Twist Fibre Craft Studio
88 High Street
Newburgh
Cupar
Fife KY14 6AQ
01337 842 843
www.twistfibrecraft.co.uk

Unlimited Colour Company
2a Latheron Lane
Ullapool
Wester-ross IV26 2XB
01854 612 844

Victoria Gibsono
The Esplanade
Lerwick
Shetland ZE1 0LL
01595 692 816

Woolcrafts Studio
Springhill Farm
Coldingham Moor Road
Eyemouth
Berwickshire TD14 5TX

The Wool Shed
Alford Heritage Centre
Mart Road
Alford
Aberdeenshire AB33 8BZ
01975 562 906

Wooly Ewe
7 Abbey Court
Kelso
Berwickshire TD5 7JA
01573 225 889

NORTHERN IRELAND

Coolwoolz
46 Mill Hill
Warringstown
County Down BT66 7QP
02838 820 202

AUSTRALIA

Calico & Ivy
1 Glyde Street
Mosman Park, WA 6012
08 9383 3794
www.calicohouse.com.au

Cleckheaton
Australian Country Spinners
314 Albert Street
Brunswick, VIC 3056
03 9380 3888
www.cleckheaton.biz

Coast Spencer Crafts
Mulgrave North, VIC 3170
03 9561 2298

The Knitting Loft
PO Box 266
Tunstall Square
East Doncaster, VIC 3109
03 9841 4818
www.knittingloft.com

The Shearing Shed
Shop 7B
Manuka Court
Bougainville Street
Manuka
Canberra, ACT 2603
02 6295 0061
www.theshearingshed.com.au

Sunspin
185 Canterbury Road
Canterbury
Melbourne, VIC 3126
03 9830 1609
www.sunspun.com.au

Tapestry Craft
50 York Street
Sydney, NSW 2000
02 9299 8588
www.tapestrycraft.com.au

Threads and More
141 Boundary Road
Bardon, QLD 4065
07 3367 0864
www.threadsandmore.
  com.au

Wool Baa
124 Bridport Street
Albert Park, VIC 3207
03 9690 6633
www.woolbaa.com.au

The Wool Shack
PO Box 228
Innaloo City
Perth, WA 6918
08 9446 6344
www.thewoolshack.com

Xotix Yarns
PO Box 1636
Kingscliff, NSW 2487
02 6677 7241
www.xotixyarns.com.au

Yarns Galore
5/25 Queens Road
Mount Pleasant, WA 6153
08 9315 3070
http://yarnsgalore.com.au

NEW ZEALAND

Accessories Stories Ltd
407 Cuba Street
Lower Hutt
Wellington
04 587 0004
www.woolworks.org

Alterknitives
PO Box 47961
Auckland
09 376 0337

Anny Blatt Handknitting Yarns
PO Box 65364
Mairangi Bay
Auckland
09 479 2043

Busy Needles
73B Victoria Street
Cambrdige

Coats Spencer Crafts
East Tamaki
09 274 0116

Accent Fibres @ Dyepot
1084 Maraekakaho Road
R.D.5
Hastings
Hawkes Bay
06 876 4233
www.dyepot.co.nz

John Q Goldingham
PO Box 45083
Epuni
Lower Hutt
04 567 4085

Knit World
189 Peterborough Street
Christchurch
03 379 2300
knitting@xtra.co.nz

Knit World
26 The Octagon
Dunedin 9001
03 477 0400

Knit World
PO Box 30045
Lower Hutt
04 586 4530
info@knitting.co.nz

Knit World
Shop 210b
Left Bank
Cuba Mall
Wellington
04 385 1918

The Stitchery
Suncourt Shopping Centre
Tamamuta Street
Taupo
07 378 9195
stitchery@xtra.co.nz

Treliske Organic Wools
2RD Roxburgh
Central Otago
03 446 6828
info@treliskeorganic.com

Wool 'n' Things
109 New Brighton Mall
New Brighton
Christchurch
03 388 3391

Wool World
26 Kelvin Street
Invercargill
03 218 8217

Yarn Barn
179 Burnett Street
Ashburton
03 308 6243

WEB RESOURCES

The Craft Yarn Council
www.craftyarncouncil.com
The Crochet Guild of America
www.crochet.org

SELECTED SUPPLIERS

www.buy-mail.co.uk
www.coatscrafts.co.uk
www.colourway.co.uk
www.coolwoolz.co.uk
www.designeryarns.uk.com
www.diamondyarns.com
www.ethknits.co.uk
www.e-yarn.com
www.handworksgallery.com
www.hantex.co.uk
www.hook-n-needle.com
www.kangaroo.uk.com
www.karpstyles.ca
www.kgctrading.com
www.knitrowan.com (features worldwide
list of stockists of Rowan yarns)
www.knittersdream.com/yarn
www.knittingfever.com
www.knitwellwools.co.uk
www.lacis.com
www.maggiescrochet.com
www.mcadirect.com
www.patternworks.com
www.patonsyarns.com
www.personalthreads.com
www.sakonnetpurls.com
www.shetland-wool-brokers-zetnet.co.uk
www.sirdar.co.uk
www.spiningayarn.com
www.theknittinggarden.com
www.upcountry.co.uk
www.yarncompany.com
www.yarnexpressions.com
www.yarnmarket.com

Index

A

AB (aurora borealis) finish 15
abbreviations 30
acrylic yarns 12
animal fibres 12
appliqué cushion 104–107

B

back post treble crochet 117
backstitch seam 34
bags:
   beaded string bag 46–47
   evening bag 52–53
   shoulder bag 48–51
   textured beaded bag 64–65
ball bands 12
beaded beanie 56–57
beaded beret 60–63
beaded crochet loop 59
beaded foundation chain 19
beaded head band 70–71
beaded hat 112–113
beaded necklace 66–67
beaded ruffle scarf 38–39
beaded string bag 46–47
beaded throw 108–109
beaded trims 120–121
beaded tunic 88–90
beads 14–15
   adding 19
   buying 14
   choosing 15
   colour-lined 15
   colours 15
   effect on tension 31
   finishes 15
   looking after 15
   opaque 15
   placing in sequence 47
   satin 15
   silver-lined 15
   sizing 15
   translucent 15
   transparent 15
beanie, beaded 56–57
beret, beaded 60–63
bikini top 91–93
blocking 32–33
box crew-neck 76–79
brooch and pendant 72–73

button loops 97
buttons 13

C

cap-sleeved wrap 94–97
cashmere yarns 12
ceylon finish 15
chain spaces 28
chains:
   foundation 19
   beaded 19
   working into 20
   number of, from hook 21
   turning 20
circular motif cushion 110–111
coasters 118–119
cobweb shrug 86–87
colours:
   beads 15
   yarns, new, joining in 24
corsage, flower pin 54–55
cotton 12
crab stitch edging 35
crochet hooks 16
cushion pads 13
cushions:
   appliqué cushion 104–107
   circular motif cushion 110–111
   floor cushion 114–117

D

daggers 14
decorative beads 14
decreases:
   beaded, in the round 63
   external 27
   internal 27
double crochet edging 35
double crochet (dc) 21
   extended (exdc) 22
double crochet seam 34
double treble crochet (dtr) 24

E

earflap hat 68–69
edge finishes 35
   beaded crochet loop 59
   crab stitch 35
   double crochet 35
evening bag 52–53
extended double crochet (exdc) 22
external decreases 27
external increases 26

F

fastening off 32
felting 48
finishing techniques 32–35
floor cushion 114–117
flower pin corsage 54–55
foundation chains 19
 working into 20
front post treble crochet 117

G

galvanized finish 15
glass beads 14, 15

H

half treble crochet (htr) 23
halter-neck top 83–85
hats:
 beaded beanie 56–57
 beaded beret 60–63
 earflap hat 68–69
head band, beaded 70–71
hooks 16
 changing position 28
 holding 18

I

increases:
 beaded, in the round 63
 external 26
 internal 26
internal decreases 27
internal increases 26
iris finish 15

J

jacket, box crew-neck 76–79
jewellery fastenings 13
jewellery wire 13

L

lace motifs, joining 29
lace work 28–29
lace-effect shawl 40–41
linen yarns 12
linked triple treble 55
loop 59
loops, button 97
lustre finish 15

M

Magatamas (teardrop beads) 14
manmade yarns 12
markers 17
materials 12–15
mats:
 beaded mat 112–113
 coasters 118–119
matte finish 15
metallic finish 15
metallic yarns 12
mohair yarns 12
motifs:
 for appliqué cushion 106–107
 for bag 51
 stitching into position 101
 for sweaters 98–101

N

necklace, beaded 66–67
needles (sewing) 17
nylon yarns 12

O

opaque beads 15
overcast seam 33

P

pashmina 44–45
patterns, understanding 30
pearl finish 15
pearls 14
pendant and brooch 72–73
picot edging 35
plies 12
polyester yarns 12
pressing 32–33

R

repeats in patterns 30
ribbon yarns 12
rounds:
 marking 25
 working in 25
row counters 17

S

sample swatch 31
satin beads 15

scarves:
 beaded ruffle scarf 38–39
 twenties-inspired scarf 58–59
scissors 17
seams 33–34
 backstitch 34
 double crochet 34
 overcast 33
 slip stitch 34
 woven 34
seed beads 14
sequins, adding 19
sewing needles 17
sewing thread 17
shaping techniques 26–27
shawls:
 lace-effect shawl 40–41
 pashmina 44–45
 shrug, cobweb 86–87
silk yarns 12
silver-lined beads 15
slash-neck vest 80–82
slip knot 18
slip stitch seam 34
slip stitch (sl st) 21
squares, joining together 41
stitches:
 basic 21–24
 counting 19
 working into 24
stuffing 13
swatch, test 31
sweaters, motifs for 98–101
synthetic yarns 12

T

tape measure 17
teardrop beads 14
tension 31
test swatch 31
textured beaded bag 64–65
throw, beaded 108–109
tools 16–17
tops:
 beaded tunic 88–90

beaded wrap 94–97
bikini top 91–93
box crew-neck 75–79
halter-neck top 83–85
motifs for 98–101
slash-neck vest 80–82
translucent beads 15
transparent beads 15
treble crochet (tr) 22–23
 back post 117
 front post 117
 half (htr) 23
trims, beaded 120–121
triple treble, linked 55
tunic, beaded 88–90
turning chains 20
Twenties-inspired scarf
 58–59

V

vegetable fibres 12
vest, slash-neck 80–82

W

weaving in ends 32
wool 12
woven seam 34
wrap, beaded 94–97
wrist warmers 42–43

Y

yarns:
 ball bands 12
 buying by weight 12
 fastening off 32
 holding 18
 new, joining 24
 novelty 12
 types 12
 weaving in ends 32
 weights 13

Z

zippers 13

Credits

Quarto would like to thank the models – Laura Caird, Claire Lithgow,
Gillian Cook and Nikki Goodwin.

All photographs and illustrations are the copyright of Quarto Publishing plc.

AUTHOR'S ACKNOWLEDGMENTS

Many thanks to Kate Buller and all the team at Rowan for their help and
support, and for the use of their gorgeous yarns and beads. Thanks also to
Irene Jackson and Lavinia Blackwall for helping me create the final projects,
and to all my friends, especially Andy for his help and encouragement.

RODALE

TOUR DE FRANCE
1999
2000 2001
2002 2003
2004
WINNER

LANCE ARMSTRONG
IMAGES OF A CHAMPION

Photography by
Graham Watson

by
Lance Armstrong

Foreword by
Robin Williams